Holy
Moments

Holy Moments

By

Elizabeth Schadrack

ISBN: 978-1-7336447-2-3 (paperback)

Also by Elizabeth Schadrack

Not Happy? Get Happy!
Pathway to Heaven
Ask, Thank, and Praise
The Art of Communication and the Power of Praise
Wisdom Is a Gift from God
What Would You Say if I Told You
PRAISE
Can Be a Form of Gun Control?

Holy Moments

Happiness is Contagious;
you can Spread it.

I Can Help!

Acknowledgments

No one makes it own their own; we all get help along the way from someone. My spiritual awaking came from Mary Kay in 1975 when I became one of her beauty consultants. I was looking for a way to bring meaning to my life and got far more than I realized at the time.

Oprah and Deepak opened my eyes to the power of meditation and the fact that I am the universe and my life is a combination of thoughts that I project. If I can see it and I can feel it and I believe it, it is entirely possible.

Al Franco, the engagement editor/opinion of *The Desert Sun* newspaper in Palm Springs, California, kickstarted me by publishing my positive thoughts in the opinion page; this raised my confidence level to a point it had never reached before. Like the song, "You raised me up to more than I could be." The compliments

I received were the encouragement I needed to write books.

Matthew Kelly confirmed my thinking about the power of prayer in his book, *The Biggest Lie in the History of Christianity.* I learned to see things as a holy moment and life is an experience to be enjoyed and a gift from God. This brings more pleasure to everyday living. He warned me that if I say this prayer, I need to get ready because I am going to be happier than I have ever been before in my life. Who does not want to be happier than they have ever been before? Thank you, Matthew, for this; I copied it, cut it up, put a happy face on it, and leave a copy of it in church for others to find. Thank you to all the people who have helped me help others find happiness in a life worth living. I appreciate you, and I am so grateful to have you in my life.

Preface

There is a large black cloud hovering over the earth, and we need to acknowledge it and deal with its symptoms; left alone, it will continue to grow. People are hurting, and they need help. Our lives have become too stressful, full of anxiety, and we are fearful about everything. These symptoms used to be exclusive to adults but have now spread to our children.

We were not meant to struggle through life. We have more power than we realize. Life can be fun. Everything that is happening right now in your life is a combination of decisions you have made in the past.

There are two elements to life: love and fear. Matthew Kelly tells us everyone who crosses the threshold of a church on Sunday is afraid of something, and they come hopeful that God will liberate them from that fear.

It took me forty-five years to realize this. I did not know whatever it was that I wanted; I must give it first. Want a friend, be a friend. When I cried out for help, I realized God does not push himself on us; he gave us a brain to think for ourselves and make our own decisions. If we want him in our lives, we must invite him.

We are born happy and laugh at the drop of a hat, and then we reach our teen years and become lost. Emptiness sets in, and we go looking for happiness. Material happiness is short-lived. A new outfit, car, home, drugs, and alcohol wear out or wear off.

Love is the light from God that fills our soul, and the only way we can ever be totally happy. Today I am happier than I have ever been before in my life, and it is because of my prayer. I received this prayer one morning after meditating.

Thank you, God, for taking over my life, directing my path, and using me to bring happiness to others. I am receiving now.

Finding the good in others, accepting them as they are, and loving them will bring all the happiness we desire and need. Encouraging our youth to volunteer will help them find their God-given gifts and, at the same time, inner peace and happiness.

I am trying to be the person I needed when I was young. I was a very needy person. I was completely void of communication skills and social skills.

When I started seeing everything as a gift from God, my whole world opened up. Now I say, "Put them in my path, God, and I will do all in my power to help them; I am so happy and grateful that you use me to bring happiness to others."

Gratitude is my attitude. The more I am grateful for, the more I get to be grateful for.

So much life to live and so little knowledge to bring about the best results. We can do better than this. The greatest game is the game of life, and it's being ignored.

A HOLY MOMENT

Early Years with Thomas

A T M Y G O O D B Y E P A R T Y B E F O R E I left for Germany, a young man at that party said things to me that made me feel so special. I do not remember what he said, but I could have run off with him that night and never looked back. He never touched me, yet his words left me on cloud nine. As I look back fifty years later, that very evening stirred something up in me; I wanted to experience that feeling again. I had never been told I was a beautiful woman and never felt so good hearing those softly spoken words.

It is like having someone look into your eyes and singing "There's No One Like You" (maybe that's why I love hearing Sarah Brightman sing that song) or the song "Love Changes Everything," and to this day, the greatest feeling comes over me just listening to the words of those songs. One line is "I believe in miracles; there's no one like you."

A restlessness sits in, way in the back of your brain, and it never leaves. You find yourself existing, not really living, longing to feel loved, for someone to hold you in his arms and tell you he loves you. My favorite movie is *Love Is a Many-Splendored Thing.* For a long time, life was doing the normal things that needed to be done: maybe paint the bedroom, change something around, wash the clothes, cook.

There is an emptiness in the pit of your stomach, and you don't know how to fill it. Your concern up to this point is what you look like on the outside.

It was important that I had breasts, so I used my Aunt Mary's breast pump to develop them. She was always having babies and had this suction thing that I used to make my breasts grow, and they did. I had beautiful breasts. My outside appearance was striking, and my inside was crying out for help. If only someone had told me it is more important to be beautiful on the inside!

How Do You Define Success?

Oprah tells us in one of her meditations that it's getting to the point where you are absolutely comfortable with yourself, and it takes work to get there. Peace comes from strength. Your greatest struggle will produce your deepest strength. If that's the case, I am the most peaceful person in the world because I struggled for the first forty-five years of my life. I was a slow learner.

INNER PEACE

What you don't know is that there is only one way to find it.

Invite God to take over your life, direct your path, and use you to bring happiness to others because that is where real happiness comes from. God could have created us without needing to breathe. But he wanted us to depend on him for something, and it took me a long time to realize this.

Life can be wonderful once we learn how to live it. Wake up each morning in a state of bliss; that's being happy for no reason. Here I am, God; what would you have me do today? Where would you have me go? What would you have me say?

A miracle took place in the upstairs bedroom of my beautiful home on Mimosa Lane one Sunday when I had reached the bottom and called out to God, crying from the depths of my soul, "Please help me! I am lost and so unhappy, and I don't know what to do." Wanting to be sure God heard me, I screamed at him in the loudest voice I could muster. "If this is all there is to life, I don't want to live it anymore! I am so lonely; I just want to die. So much life to live, and so little knowledge about how to live it to get the best results."

President Lincoln once said, "I have been driven to my knees many times by the overwhelming conviction that I had no place else to go."

AMAZING GRACE

The greatest game is the game of life and how to get the most out of it. "Amazing Grace" keeps popping up in my life. I always related that song with a white man with a large boat transporting slaves, human beings, to the United States for sale, and one day God talked to him, and his conscience got the best of him, and he stopped.

Lately as I think about it, I can relate it to myself:

> Amazing grace, how sweet the sound,
> that saved a wretch like me.
> I once was lost, but now am found;
> was blind, but now I see.
> How precious did that grace appear,
> the hour I first believed.
> That is the magic line, the hour I first believed.

Can we not relate that to all the people on drugs, with addiction of any kind? I was blind, and now I see. I was blind to a way of living. That should become our recovery song.

After that day, my whole world opened up. We take "ask and you shall receive" lightly, but all you need to do is ask.

A HOLY MOMENT

ASK, AND YOU SHALL RECEIVE.

God does not push himself on anyone; he must be invited in.

A *holy moment* like none other.

You never know when a favor you are doing for someone else turns out to be the best thing that ever happens to you. As a young person going to the movies, I saw the young and restless driving their convertibles on roads lined with flowering shrubs and thought, *How beautiful is that?* California was the place to be if you wanted to become a movie star, and in my eyes, they were very special people, rich and knowing how to be happy. I wanted to live like they did.

I never wanted to go to California as many do. The fear of an earthquake kept me away, having seen pictures on the cover of *LIFE* magazine where the earth opens up, and you could fall into those big cracks. Boredom replaced the fear, and little did I know that God had a hand in the whole process.

Before long, my house sold. I was on my way to California to meet my cousin. What I did not know was there was a man there waiting for me, and he was lost too. He really needed me, having lost his son in a surfing accident and his wife to ovarian cancer.

Now when I hear Sarah Brightman sing "Just Show Me How to Love You," I can go back to the first time I met him and all the warm feelings I had when he said, "I am the loneliest man in the world." Goose bumps ran up and down my body. A German and a gentleman. Born in the month of March, so he was a Pisces, and Scorpios get along well with Pisces. This was a man who needed the love and companionship of a woman, and even though he was capable of performing the sex act, his interest was in me as a person, not my body.

I knew the first night I met him God had answered my prayers because I asked for someone who needed me. I guess to be needed was to be accepted since I was not an educated person; I wanted someone to love me just as I was.

Prayers Are Answered

MY PRAYERS WERE ANSWERED, AND I could not sleep that night. We talked all night, God and me, and I thanked him for sending me clear across the country to this clean, honest man who needed me. You see, that was my prayer: send me someone who needs me, and he doesn't have to be handsome or rich—just clean, honest, and needs me. No one on this earth could have needed me more.

What I got was a very handsome, wealthy, clean, honest man who drank like a fish and smoked like a train but was in desperate need of a wife. He never drank anything until he lost his twenty-three-year-old son in a surfing accident in Maui, but he had been a smoker for many years.

There comes a time in one's life when we are not content just being married; we need to be appreciated, kissed goodbye in the morning, appreciated for who we are, asked "How was your day?" and communicated with.

My First Marriage to Thomas

Having been married to a man from a broken home, I realize that life is different in many ways, so I'm not criticizing him; he was a good man. I'm just saying there has to be more to life than "What's for dinner tonight?" and "Did you wash my clothes today?" As I did not have any cooking skills, it was not easy coming up with something different for dinner each night. And I never heard, "Hm, this is good. Thank you. I really appreciate all you do for me, You look great in that outfit. I am so proud of you." We never thanked each other for anything. When you live like this, you have a limited desire to do better or more. Appreciation plays a large role in a lasting marriage.

Love is the desire to do with and for without expecting anything in return, and appreciation will set you apart from the rest of the world. A compliment is a moment of happiness in another person's life. Did he think if he complimented me I would get a big head and leave him?

What did I know? I just wanted to get married. All my friends were getting married and having children, so why not me too? I married the first person who asked me. I think I told him I wanted to be married, so he asked me.

He was in the service, so this offered some excitement to my life. I left Maryland and moved to Texas. I took the train for a two-day trip, and I loved it. I transferred with the telephone company. We lived in Temple, Texas, for nine months before Thomas was shipped out to Germany. Fort Hood was a half-hour drive for him.

It was 1951, and I was so excited. I was on my way to Germany to join my husband and was taking our little eight-month-old son whom he had never seen. He would be happy to see this beautiful child because his mother wrote him and said, "He is a beautiful child, but one of his eyes is bigger than the other." What a stupid thing to write to your son! Is there any question why I never got along with this woman?

I never thought I would ever be leaving this country. The name of this ship was the *La Guardia*, a troop ship, and there were about six women in each room in bunk beds, and all of us had a child or two with us. One night we encountered a storm. We didn't know it until we went to the bathroom, and there was a lot of vomiting going on in there—and a lot to be cleaned up the next morning.

Breakfast was served on wet tablecloths so our plates would not slide, and then we saw men walking up and down the deck with these big things we learned later were compasses. It turned out that due to the storm, we were lost at sea. Very interesting. I think it took us about ten days to arrive in Bremerhaven, Germany.

We arrived in the night, and it seemed that we got off the ship and onto a train. When you are traveling like this, you are kind of hustled like cattle. No one is giving you any directions like, "We have arrived in Bremerhaven, Germany, and now we are going to board a train to Nuremberg." It was, "Get your stuff together because you are going to Nuremberg!" and off we went to Nuremberg.

MY NEW FRIEND ARNELL

I had taken a woman named Arnell under my wing. It was her decision; after all, in her eyes, I was a world traveler because I was from Maryland, traveled to Texas and then to New York, and now to Germany. She remained under my wing.

Our husbands were stationed at Fort Hood in Klein, Texas. She had never left Texas before, and she said to me, "I hope you like me because I have decided that I am going to stay with you, if you don't mind." She stayed with me; we took turns going to the kitchen in the night to get warm milk for our babies.

We got on the train, and there she was in my compartment again. There was hardly enough room for one, but she was going to stay there, and the strangest thing happened. I never knew this woman before—I had met her in New York—and when we arrived in Nuremberg, our husbands had come in the same car to pick us up! They already knew each other. We talked about that for years to come.

A funny thing happened on that troop ship. When it was my turn to go to the kitchen for milk for our sons, I invariably would end up going down the wrong end of the ship. One end went downstairs to the kitchen; the other end went to the men's showers. So there I was, headed down the steps, and I usually moved pretty fast. And boom! Before I got to the bottom, all of a sudden I saw all these naked men showering. I turned and hotfooted it up the steps again and found my way down to the other end, but there did not seem to be any markings of any kind to say, "This way to the kitchen," so that didn't happen just one time. This happened to me two or three times, and finally I was headed down the steps one night. I looked up, and someone had posted a sign at the top of the steps that read MEN'S SHOWERS. I think they were getting tired of seeing this woman coming down with the baby bottles. That was very much appreciated because I didn't like it either; even though I had been alone for a long time and without a husband, I wasn't really enjoying watching these men washing themselves.

We had arrived in Nuremberg, and it was just like you see—all of these GIs hanging out of the train when they arrive home. That's the way we were: women and children hanging out of the windows and our men out on the platform. And of course it was very exciting for them because a lot of them had never seen these babies we were bringing to them. I remember the first few days of my son's experience with his father. He seemed to be frightened of him; he had never seen this man before, and he wasn't having anything to do with him.

We were in this really big apartment, an old German officer's quarters, and we would be there for about six months while our brand-new apartments were being finished in an area called Baumholder. It was quite a bit south of Nuremberg, and I think it was about an eight-hour drive by car. We had this big, beautiful apartment on the second floor. It had wide circular cement steps. An old skeleton key like they used in the olden days opened up the door to a big living room with a potbelly stove, a big kitchen, two big bedrooms, and a very large bathroom with a big tub. It was referred to as "the Swinenow Casern." I don't know if that's a name the GIs gave it because the word *swine* is the word for "pig," and that is not too nice, but actually it was the old German officers' quarters in the days of the war. It was very nice, and we were very comfortable.

Our housekeeper did all of our laundry in that bathtub on a washboard, bent over. She had the most interesting way of hanging clothes; she ran two clotheslines in that extra bedroom, and instead of hanging them side by side as we do, she hung the clothes from one side of the rope to the other, and she hung our whole week's laundry in that room. I could not believe it! And nothing ever dripped on the floor; it was just wonderful. Her name was Susie, and we loved her.

It started getting cold in August, and unbeknownst to me, there was a man who had a key to our apartment. He came in and started the fires in our potbelly stoves. We referred to him as our fireman. I don't remember anyone telling me that a fireman was going to come in and out of our apartment the first thing every morning, in the middle of the day, and again at night, and that he was going to stoke the fire in these two potbelly stoves.

I was frightened to death of him. He did not speak English, and he had a lot of scars on his face like pockmarks. Someone told me he that he was Russian. Well, I was never afraid of Russians or Germans, but since I could not communicate with this man, I had a fear of him, and there were no communications between the two of us.

He unlocked the door, came in, stoked the fire, and then left. I don't think he said hello, goodbye, kiss my foot, or anything. A funny thing happened that was frightening to me. I had lived in the country in Maryland, and we never locked our doors; I don't think we had keys for our doors. I had never been out of the state of Maryland until I went to Texas. Having transferred with my job, we lived in Temple, Texas, and my husband only came home on weekends, so I was frightened there too.

I went to bed with a hammer under my pillow, but I made sure all the doors were locked. It was necessary for me to keep working because a serviceman didn't make that much money—not that we needed that much money because I'm not a big spender.

The circus was in town. They were shutting down for the winter, and someone had given them permission to park their trucks and their paraphernalia in the parking lot of this apartment complex. We were told this was the circus and they would be there for the winter.

One night I had a knock on my door, and it was dark outside. There was no telephone, so I couldn't call anyone, and my first thought was, *My friends don't come out at night.* I was just going to wait until I heard footsteps going down the stairs; then I would look through the big keyhole to see who it was. If it was someone I knew, I would call to them and open the door; if it wasn't, I would just pretend I was not here.

I waited a minute or two. I didn't hear any footsteps, but I thought they must be on their way down, and I didn't want to take a chance of missing them, so I got down and looked in the keyhole. I saw the biggest eyeball you ever want to see looking back at me! That scared me out of my wits. Then she said to me, "*Ine stick broad bitter?*" and I thought, *What on earth is she saying to me? Ine stick broad bitter.* "A piece of bread, please." To this day, it hurts me to think I never gave that old woman a piece of bread. My goodness, if I had known then and not been so frightened, I would have given her a whole loaf of bread, but she scared the living devil out of me, and that was the last time I have ever looked through a keyhole. I made sure I found the key to that door and left it in the keyhole; I just stuck it there on the inside so no one could look in again. When the fireman came in the morning, he had to push the key through the other side so he could get in. This apartment complex we were living in was in a little town called Fürth. It was just a short distance outside of Nuremberg, and when I say "short distance," we didn't have a vehicle— our husbands had our vehicles—so it was about a ten-minute ride on the trolley.

I shipped my car over there, and we went to Bremerhaven to pick it up. I refer to our vehicle as "mine" because I wrecked the one my husband left me, so I bought another one, a 1951 black Plymouth. He was not happy about that because we had a classic Pontiac, which he loved. I forgot to check the antifreeze, and the block froze up and cracked.

Arnell and I would take the little trolley (street-car), and it only took us ten minutes to get to down-town Nuremberg where all the department stores were. I enjoyed speaking the little German I knew. I wanted the people there to think I was a German, and the first thing I learned from Susie was how to say, "Excuse me, please," and then I enjoyed see-ing the faces of the Germans. When I wanted to get off the trolley, I would say, "*Entschuldigen sie bitte*," which means, "Excuse me, please." I never went into town by myself; Arnell and I always went together, and it was a funny thing—she always decided she wanted to go into town when Susie was at my house doing my laundry and she wanted to drop her little boy off. He was one month younger than mine. His name was Billie Lynn, and Susie could not get anything done; she had two little boys to watch. We were off having a good time, and I didn't give much thought to it until after a couple of times. I knew that Susie had her hands full with two little boys, and I couldn't expect her to do the laundry and clean the house.

While we were running around in the stores, we were just playing Miss Big Shot. We would go to the fur coat department and laugh and try on the fur coats. Arnell wanted a fur coat; she wasn't fat, but she was heavier than me. I was very thin, and when she put on a coat, she looked like a bear, but we were just silly women having the best time.

When we entered this big department store, it had a terrible odor because they had a fish counter that sold all kinds of smoked fish, and next to it, they had a soap counter where you bought all your soap. The combination of smelling the fish and the soap was just unbearable.

We almost had to hold our noses until we could get up to the next floor, and I don't remember either one of us ever buying one thing in that department store. We would just go. It was an outing for us just to have fun, and of course we didn't understand the language, so we couldn't hear what the people were saying. Maybe they were saying things that were not nice about us for the way we were acting. That's what's nice about not understanding: If someone is saying something ugly, you don't hear it, but the German people are very nice, and they were probably just laughing at those two silly girls, laughing all the time in a ridiculous way.

It was November, and my little baby's birthday is November 16; his father's birthday is November 11, and mine is November 17. He was born fifteen minutes before midnight, and I was born in the afternoon before my mother's birthday, which was November 18. Time to make a birthday cake! While I was working for the telephone company in Temple, one of my friends brought me a piece of the most wonderful cake I had ever eaten—banana nut cake with banana nut icing. She gave me the recipe; the only cake I'd ever had in my life was a yellow cake or a marble cake. I thought I would treat us all, and I made this banana nut cake with banana nut icing, and I had my friend Arnell and her husband and little boy over for dinner that night. I thought they would leave the earth when I served them that cake. It was out of this world. Well, of course, Billy Groom, whose job in the service was a cook, right away wanted the recipe for that cake so he could make it himself. He said, "I am going to eat the whole thing myself!" It was so good.

LEAVING FOR BAUMHOLDER

It was February now, and it was time for us to leave. Our new quarters were finished, and we were heading to Baumholder. We had our inspection; someone had to come and inspect your quarters when you left to be sure that all of the silverware was there and everything was intact.

We packed our 1951 Plymouth, and we were off. It was winter, and winter in Germany is really winter. I remember our little son, Tom, was standing on the seat between his father and me, and we were going down the road. All of a sudden, we were in a blizzard. It was snowing so hard, and the wind was blowing. We looked up, and there was a man in the middle of the road. We couldn't go very fast. Had we been able to go at any speed, we would have run over him.

Saved in a Snow Storm

HE STOPPED US AND RECOMMENDED we turn around: "You can't get through; there is a mile of cars over in the ditch on the side of the road because you can't see the road." Snow was blowing so hard that we could not see anything. So my husband turned around, and we took another route. The man told him where to go; men know how to tell you where to go, right? But this man was nice, and he told him which route to look for and directed us the best he could. So we were on our way to Baumholder, and we arrived.

Now we had a third-floor apartment, and it was all brand new. It had a darling desk with a chair, really pleasant living room furniture, a sofa, two chairs, lamps, a coffee table, and a appealing kitchen. The kitchen had a built-in bench around a round table, and it had a great stove, a nice bathroom, two bedrooms, silverware, dishes, pots, and pans. We were all set in our new apartment.

It was very special living in Baumholder. We could walk down to the play area where the children had swings and a sliding board, and I remember we bought our little son a tricycle that he could ride on the sidewalk. One day I took him down after our daughter had been born; I had just come home from the hospital with her.

He took off on that tricycle as fast as his little legs would go. The sidewalk slanted downhill, and he could not stop. If he could, he did not want to, and I knew when he reached the bottom of the hill, he would flip over into oncoming traffic. It was just a two-lane road, but people drove pretty fast. He was two years old now, and he was like a caged animal just turned loose going down that hill. I was hollering, "Stop! Stop!" I didn't know if he could stop; all he seemed to know how to do was go forward.

There were some women sitting out on the steps, and I handed them my baby and went running after him. She was just two weeks old at the most, and when he reached the bottom of the road, his little tricycle turned over with him right into the road. Luckily, the cars coming saw him, and no one hit him before I could gather him up, but oh my goodness, I have never been so frightened in my life!

That was a *holy moment* before I knew there was such a thing.

I could see this child on this little tricycle dumping into that road and a car hitting him and that was the end of my son. He was an adorable child; he is still a good-looking young man, but he was the cutest little boy you would ever want to see. Baumholder was fun; I loved to walk into the little town where the shops were and don't remember ever buying anything except a cuckoo clock and beer steins because they had little naked ladies in the handles, and we thought they would be nice to take home as gifts for our friends.

A number of us became pregnant, so our government sent an ob-gyn doctor over from Arkansas. *Wow,* was he ever good-looking! The kind of guy who looks like he is right off the farm. We considered staying pregnant, but that did not happen. On one of my visits I asked him, "Since there is only one doctor, what happens if two of us decide to deliver at the same time?" Guess what? I was the second person ready to deliver, and it was not that much of a problem; another doctor delivered my baby.

We also had a beer wagon. Instead of having

a milk truck, we had a beer wagon and had beer delivered to the door. These beer bottles were so neat! You could open the bottle and drink what you wanted, then close it, and it snapped with a springlike wire on top that kept the beer fresh. That was very interesting; I had never seen beer distributed like that in our country.

The only thing we ever complained about when we lived there was the odor of the honey wagon. They collected human waste and sprayed it over the fields. I don't know how they collected it, but they did, and they put it in a big barrel, and the horses pulled it. Then they sprayed it on their crops. The United States government provided us with pills, and we were to wash our vegetables in water with these pills. I don't ever remember anyone getting sick, so I guess it worked, or maybe it wasn't as dangerous as we thought.

In time, that marriage fell apart. It lasted about twelve years. That empty, restless feeling grows; it's like a black cloud hovering over you, and you don't know how to remove it. You are young, infatuated with wealth and looks. Your happiness comes in spurts, from a new dress, a car—material things that wear out or off.

You just move through the day, never showing appreciation for what others do for you, never writing thank-you notes, ready for a confrontation, saying hurtful things. I like the way Oprah refers to it: "Just trying to make it through the day."

So alone with no real friends and so lonely, I reached out to Mary Kay Cosmetics for an opportunity to meet people. What I did not know was I was going to find spiritually. Your first thought in sales should be *How can I help this person?* You allow the person to sell themselves by filling their need. Zig Ziglar was a great teacher of this idea, and Mary Kay had him as one of our guest speakers. He was a great guy. I love this saying of his: "If you see someone without a smile, give them yours."

A Holy Moment

Mary Kay Ash was responsible for turning my life around.

I didn't know squat about cosmetics; at forty-seven years old, I never wore cosmetics. I wanted to be a part of something and have meaning to my life. I worked for IBM, but that was work, and work is not spiritually fulfilling.

I found it was the turning point in my life, spiritually. Mary Kay was a very spiritual person, and it was contagious, and I caught it. I learned the importance of listening, caring about others, writing thank-you notes, showing appreciation for what others do for you, and being grateful for the people in my life.

Up until that point, all my thinking was about myself. I had been dating a very handsome man. I was infatuated with his looks, his Jaguar, weekends on his boat, and his ability to take me places I had never been—Paris, Spain—and that was not working.

THE STRUGGLES OF LIFE

The call came from my cousin Pat, who lived in Pennsylvania. I was living in Silver Spring, Maryland, in the suburbs of Washington, DC. She went on to say, "I'm renting my house out and relocating to California, and I'm wondering if you would go with me." I agreed to do so, but it was not on my bucket list of things to do or places to go. Her only son, Greg, lived there with his wife, Carrie, and she was asking herself, "Why am I living here?" She wanted to be where she could see her son once in a while; after all, he was all she had.

I had just quit my job with IBM and sold my house. Everything is a learning experience, and this turned out to be one as well. First you sell your house; then you quit your job. Otherwise, you have no money to pay the bills, and the house will get cold when the gas gets turned off, and it is not easy to sell a cold house.

The timing was perfect for a trip. My two children were out on their own now. What did I need with a big two-story colonial house? I'm only one little person; I can live anywhere. I was forty-seven years old and lonely—so lonely, I could have just died.

My life had been nothing but one big struggle. When I went to the grocery store, I had to count as I went along to be sure I had enough money when I got to the cashier so I wouldn't be embarrassed for lack of funds.

The house was beautiful, and anyone would be happy living there except me. It had been $27,000 brand new in 1963, with three bedrooms and two baths upstairs and a living room, dining room, family room, kitchen, laundry room, and half bath downstairs. There was a wood-burning fireplace in the family room. It was the nicest house I had ever lived in up until that point; I should have been happy. I loved it when I moved in, but it became a financial struggle. I ate, drank, and slept struggle; it was all I ever knew. And as I said, stuff wears out or off.

It took me a long time to learn that happiness does not come from stuff. I was constantly doing things to that house. Buying magazines for ideas—*House Beautiful, Better Homes and Gardens*—saving up the money to create any idea I thought would make our home more beautiful. It was good that I had to wait before I could do some of these projects because often I changed my mind.

My son, Thomas, commented to me one day, "Every time you do something, you sit for an hour and look at it." It was true; I sat for hours and looked at it because that was bringing me happiness.

Some of my fondest memories were the blue onion wallpaper on the kitchen wall, and then I found a blue fabric and created a pleated drape for the sliding glass door. I don't know where this knowledge came from to make a drape, but I did it. The fabric store must have instructed me on how to do it.

The family room was one of my favorite rooms in this home. I hired a man to build a floor-to-ceiling bookcase on one wall. I saw this in one of the magazines, and I put the television in the middle of it and greenery on a couple of shelves with the leaves cascading down. I found a bust of Kennedy, added that, and shopped garage sales for books. It was beautiful. It had red carpet, a black leather sofa, a black leather beanbag in front of the fireplace, black-and-white paisley curtains on the windows, and two high-back chairs covered in the same paisley material. It was a beautiful room.

Things didn't always turn out beautifully, like the wallpaper job I did in the stairwell. Not knowing the first thing about hanging wallpaper, I set out to do it myself. I figured out a way to lean the ladder back against the steps so I could reach the top; I wet the paper and used a special brush to smooth it out. The only problem was when the heat came on in the winter, the paper came down. There was a sizing step in the preparation I was not aware of. That job turned out to be expensive; I had to hire someone to remove the paper and clean the wall.

Having very tall poplar trees in the backyard presented me with another problem: the leaves filled up the gutters, and when it rained, the water overflowed the gutters and flooded the basement. I don't like water problems, and dipping water out of a basement is hard, time-consuming work. Off to Lowe's for a solution, and it was screening to be installed under the roofing. How do I get up there to do this job? Being single presents many challenges. There is only one way: use the ladder to get to the top of the carport roof, pull the ladder up to you, and use it to get to the next roof.

Now you are on top looking down three stories, and you don't like heights. You must walk very carefully to the edge of the roof, remove the old leaves, lift the roofing, and install these sheets of screening under the roofing and over the gutter. *Wow!* It has to be done, and someone has to do it. It is definitely not the time to be wearing your leather-soled shoes. And this happened before I learned to meditate!

Learning to Meditate

SATURDAY NIGHTS I SPENT ON the beanbag in front of the fireplace watching television. God was after me in those days, but I was not aware of it. Johnny Carson had the guru from India, Maharishi Mahesh Yogi, on one night talking about meditation and the results of it. He rented houses in different areas and had a group of young people teaching this process. I contacted the group in my area and was informed to arrive with a piece of fruit and flowers. Upon arrival, I was taken to a private room and given my own special mantra. This was the beginning of a new life for me; things just kept getting better.

I was raised by my grandparents, and they struggled all their lives. I could have measured their level of happiness in a thimble. We lived in a house without running water and with no inside plumbing, and the winters get very cold in Maryland. Drinking water was gathered in a bucket by my grandfather each day.

We did have electricity, however, and my grandparents were able to listen to the radio. I remember hearing *As the World Turns, The Young and the Restless,* and *Fibber McGee and Molly. Amos 'n' Andy* was a favorite; listening to soap operas and baseball was their life.

They were wonderful people. They raised seven children of their own, five girls and two boys. Then the worst thing that can happen to grandparents happened to them: their daughter Elizabeth died. She had strep throat, and the doctor lanced the blisters, not knowing it would kill her; it went into her bloodstream. There were four children under the age of five to be raised. Bradley, the father of these children, was twenty-three years old, and my brothers tell me he left the day of the funeral. I was only three months at this time, so I have no recollection.

When I think about my grandmother, I can still laugh at her comment when I was about six years old. Uncle Frank, her youngest child, had already left home before our mother died. He was bringing his girlfriends out with him to visit his mother and father, and they always treated me with kindness, brushed my hair, and hugged me, and I loved it. One of them gave me a tube of lipstick, and in those days, lipstick was one color: bright red. Never having seen anyone apply lipstick, I applied it and took on the appearance of a clown. One look at me and my grandmother said, "My word, child, your mouth looks like a blackbird's ass in pokeberry time!" Where did that come from? Given an opportunity to ask her now, I would like to know how many blackbirds' asses she had seen, and what time of year is pokeberry time?

I've often wished I could have shown them some real life, treated them to a dinner at a special restaurant, or shown some appreciation of all they did for me and my brothers, but by the time I was able to do so, they were dead.

Arriving in Los Angles—Cousin Pat from Pennsylvania

I flew into Los Angeles from Washington, DC, and Pat flew in from Pennsylvania. We met at a hotel, and she went immediately to a used car lot and bought a car. From there we went to a small apartment she had rented prior to our arrival. There was no furniture, just a blow-up mattress on the floor, which was just fine.

Our plan was to hit the road, and the first stop would be Three Rivers to visit her son, Greg, and her daughter-in-law, Carrie, for a few days. Greg was working with the California forestry service, and Carrie was a school teacher. We learned a lot about *widow-makers* from Greg, a term I had never heard before. It was due to the dangers of the job. Trees can fall and kill you if you are not careful. They both seemed so happy to have found each other, and I was happy for them.

If you have not traveled the Number 1 highway, you need to add it to your bucket list. I promise you will be happy you did. The ocean is on one side and the mountains on the other. Waves pound into large rocks rising up out of the ocean, and the spray of the water at the edge of the road is a beautiful sight to see, especially in the Mendocino area. I love the ocean and the tranquility it brings about in me. Be sure to stop at Big Sur and visit Nepenthe; go up top and have coffee or wine, and look out over the beautiful area. Enjoy the big, beautiful Steller's jays and their loud squawking.

We drove as far north as Fort Bragg (no, not North Carolina—California). It surprised me too; I had never heard of this before. We were returning to Santa Monica on Sunday afternoon where Pat had her new digs. It was dinnertime, and she said that if I saw a place I might like to stop for dinner, I should shout. I shouted, "We just passed a place that looks delightful, right on the ocean, and you could see the waves pounding the rocks in front of it. The Nantucket Light in Malibu." She whipped the car around, and we entered the restaurant.

The waitress greeted us and informed us there would be a half-hour wait. No problem; we would wait. I was standing there waiting in my Victorian petticoat. I was into Victorian clothes at that time; it was a straight white sleeveless dress with no form, and it had flowers embroidered across the top. I thought it was pretty. As I recall that time in my life, the clothes I was wearing were definitely a change from my IBM attire. Maybe an after-retirement rebellion, you think?

As we stood at the entrance to the bar bustling with people, waiting our turn, Pat struck up a conversation with Karl Malden, the actor from *The Streets of San Francisco*. I was mesmerized by the beauty of this place and was not paying any attention to what she was saying, but knowing he was from Pennsylvania, I assume she said it looked like Pennsylvania was being well represented there that day.

At the Nantucket Light

THIS IS WHERE IT GETS good. The waitress approached and said, "The gentleman at that table with the couple wants to know if you two ladies would like to join them for dinner." Two forty-seven-year-olds being asked to join anyone for dinner would say *yes*.

I have no idea what I said or talked about because I had no communication skills at that time. I probably talked about myself, how wonderful I am. I worked for IBM, and IBMers think they are a special breed. A real country bumpkin is the best way I would describe myself. Being invited anywhere by anyone, I would become stressed, and my first thought was, *What will I talk about?* I had not read Dale Carnegie's book *How to Win Friends and Influence People* at that time and did not know the importance of bringing people out by asking proper questions and showing an interest in them.

As I write these words, I am reminded this is why I write today. I am trying to be the person I needed when I was young, and I was a very needy person, completely void of communication skills and social skills.

The most rewarding relationship in my life turned out to be the one I had with Heinzel. He was exactly what I needed when I needed it. I was always relaxed just being myself with him. He saw me as an intelligent, uneducated person with a desire to learn, and he was going to be my teacher. The desire was so strong that I decided to put myself through finishing school. He taught me about worldly things—the Magna Carta, world wars—but I needed to know how to set a proper table, communicate, and behave in a manner others would want to emulate.

On Castellammare Drive

HE WAS BORN HEINRICH PETER Drusedau to Marie geb.Verschragen of Utrecht Holland and Kaufmann Heinrich Drusedau of Bremerhaven, Germany; he became Henry Peter Drusedau at the time of his American citizenship.

After our dinner at the Nantucket Light, Heinzel invited all of us back to his home for after-dinner drinks. His home was beautiful, just a short distance from the Nantucket Light in the Pacific Palisades, right on the ocean with a short walk down the hill to the beach. Spiral steps led to the front door with a black iron railing. There was a flagstone patio behind a circle of very tall Italian cypress trees and a beautiful fountain with water coming out of the top of an angel to calm the nerves.

When we entered his home, he invited me to sit on the hearth of his fireplace away from the others. It was a floor-to-ceiling stone work of art that had been created by an Italian stone master. I don't remember being asked if I wanted a drink, and he didn't drink anything either. We talked about Germany. I had lived in Germany for three years with my now ex-husband who was an American serviceman. Heinzel was born, raised, and educated in Bremerhaven, a seaport that happened to be the place we entered by ship when I arrived to join my husband. I remembered it so well.

He told me he had to join some form of service at a certain age, and he decided on the air force. His thinking was, up there, no one knows what you are doing, and he said there was no way he could kill another person. His brother was a member of the SS; he was caught and was killed. He never knew the details of his death but never forgot his father's remark: "Why wasn't it you that got killed instead of him?" He shared so much about the war with me and how he met his wife, Ursula, when she was a nurse, how he applied for a job in this country but could not get in because they were only allowing Jewish people to migrate at that time.

He excepted an invitation to come to Canada to create a fish-meal plant. He had been selling fish after the war but knew nothing about creating a fish-meal plant. He would have to learn because he wanted to get out of Bremerhaven. He relocated to Canada with Ursula and their five-year-old son, Peter, and lived there for a number of years. His favorite song was "A Sentimental Journey."

Just as I was being enticed by cartoons of road-runners and young people driving convertibles in the movies, Heinzel and Ursula were longing to go to the place they were seeing in magazines: beautiful, sunny southern California where it is warm. They sold their home, packed what they could in their car, and left for California, the land of tall, flowering trees, large clusters of blue flowers hanging from them like bunches of grapes. The leaves looked more like ferns than the leaves I was used to seeing. We did not have these trees in Maryland. They have a Mexican name, and some of us call them jacaranda, but the proper pronunciation is with an *H*, or so I am told.

Flowering shrubs line the streets; there are pink and white blooming oleanders in the medians of the freeways and hot-pink bougainvillea climbing the walls everywhere you look. The first time I read the word *bougainvillea* was in the book *The Thorn Birds*, which took place in Australia, so I was very surprised to see them growing here in California.

At the time I met Heinzel, he had lost his wife, Ursula, to ovarian cancer and his son, Peter, had died in a surfing accident in Maui. Peter was about to graduate from Berkeley and had gone to Maui with friends to surf. It is a known fact the surf gets wicked, and a number of Berkeley students had already died surfing there.

Heinzel received the call from one of Peter's friends saying that Peter was missing.

"What do you mean Peter is missing? How could he be missing?"

The young lady went on to say, "We had a really bad storm here yesterday, and the helicopters were picking up those of us who could hold on to a rope, and the last we saw of Peter, he was floating out to sea on top of the water, and we can't find him now."

His only son gone, and it was difficult to accept without being able to see him dead.

He flew to Maui and remained there for two weeks looking for Peter, but Peter was not to be found. His tall, six-foot-two, handsome son was not going to come home ever again. It had been several years since Peter's disappearance and presumed death and one year since Ursula's death when I met Heinzel, sitting there beside him on the hearth of his fireplace listening to him tell me about his life then and what it had become now. This was when he turned to me and said, "I am the loneliest man in the world." *Wow!* Goose bumps still run up and down my body relating to that night.

That was a *holy moment* like none other. I knew my prayers were being answered, and God had sent me someone very special because, as I told him, he is the only one who knows the kind of man I can get along with. I knew that night, as I lay on the floor on Pat's blow-up mattress, I was going to marry that man.

I was so excited I could not sleep; I put myself in his house mentally. I saw myself walking down to the beach after he left for work, and I thought about what my friends and family would say about me marrying this man and living in California. The thinking is, if you can see it, and you can feel it and you can believe it, it's possible. I am a *believer!*

I remained in California for a week or so and saw him every night. Then I told him I had to return home; I had just sold my home and had some loose ends to tie up. That was a little white lie. The truth was, I had promised my friend Ellie I would go to an Engelbert Humperdinck concert with her. She had bought the tickets and invited me, and I did not want to disappoint her. One must be tactful at times like this, especially when the relationship is so fresh.

He accepted the facts and asked if I would leave a pair of my shoes at his front door as a reminder of my return. I did, and to my surprise, he gave me a thousand dollars in cash. I never asked why; I just assumed it was to ensure my return.

What I did not know was he had a housekeeper coming twice a week. Espe was a stocky Mexican woman with so much love in her heart, and she kept the house clean and did his laundry. She had been hired and trained by Ursula because she knew Heinzel would need someone when she was no longer in the picture. She offered to cook for him, too, but he turned her down as she was Mexican. He was not fond of Mexican food. Since he was a member of the Los Angeles Athletic Club, he ate his main meal at noon at the club.

Who would have thought this German would come to this country; get a job with the Union Bank, whose president is Jewish; be asked by an American president, Ronald Reagan, to come to Washington, DC, for three months to investigate the Small Business Administration and become a personal friend of Jimmy Roosevelt, whose father was responsible for us getting in the second World War with Germany, in which he was a pilot? Seeing pictures of the two of them together, you can see they had a fondness for each other.

I'm not sure how many years Heinzel worked for the Union Bank, but I do know he was a very valuable employee. He had an office in downtown Los Angles with numerous employees and another office in San Francisco. With Union Bank considered a business bank, Heinzel was responsible for all the loans given out in the state of California by the bank.

The End of the Struggle

FOR THE FIRST TIME IN my life, I felt like Cinderella; my struggle had finally come to an end. I had nothing to do, and nothing was expected of me. We had a gardener, but I found things I could do in the garden. I polished the flagstone patio floor, painted the black rail leading to the front door, and cooked fish for dinner. Heinzel loved fish, and Maryland girls know how to cook fish. He called me on his ham radio and let me know when he was within fifteen minutes of home so I could have dinner waiting for him. There were no cell phones in those days.

Ursula had little rubber plants hanging under the pergola in our backyard, and I replaced them with large pots of impatiens and fuchsias in many colors, and they were beautiful. They loved the mist in the ocean air and grew so well. It turned out to be the selling feature when it came time to sell the house. The buyer had one stipulation, and that was that the hanging garden stay just as it was.

THE GARDEN ROOM

One of my favorite rooms was the little room we referred to as the garden room. This room had a beautiful walnut desk sitting in front of a wall of small pane glass windows and a lime-green glass lamp sitting at one end, and you looked out into a garden of hanging baskets. A large floor-to-ceiling window was on the left, and a glass door on the right provided lots of light. I loved sitting there on a rainy day, writing letters back home to family and friends. It was just the right place to enjoy the garden. An *L*-shaped sofa of brown tweed fabric and a long wooden coffee table completed the room.

Volunteering made me feel special.

After a while, I ran out of things to do and, not wanting to sit and watch Espe work, I volunteered at Saint John's Hospital in Santa Monica. I loved every minute of it; wearing my white nurse's dress and nurse's shoes made me feel special. After work, I stopped by the fish market on Colorado Avenue and picked up something for dinner. What a fish market! I had never seen anything like it before.

Volunteering gave me something to talk about since Heinzel did not know my family or friends; it isn't much fun hearing about people you don't know. He told me Hollywood people don't like to be recognized, and a lot of them went to that hospital, so if and when I saw them while working at the hospital, I should pretend I didn't know who they were. Well, that makes you look pretty stupid, right?

There I was in the elevator with Lorne Green, just the two of us. The elevator stopped and a young lady got on. Assuming we were together, she looked at me and said, "*Bonanza?*" and I just shrugged my shoulders as if to say, "I don't know." It felt pretty silly doing that since I had watched *Bonanza* for years—Dan Blocker, known as Hoss Cartwright, felt like a family member—and I told Heinzel that night I wasn't doing that again. Lorne Green must have thought this woman had been living in a cave. Give me the chance now, and I would give him a big hug and tell him how much I loved his show. Since when do I allow a German to tell me how to act in my own country?

Across the street from our home on Castellammare Drive lived a darling woman named Mary Van Lear, and she taught piano. What a pleasure to listen to her recordings of classical piano when you arrived at her door! Heinzel told me that her husband had been a special person in the service, and every morning, he had played reveille on his trumpet. I was sorry I had missed that; he had passed before I arrived.

SOCIAL SKILLS

I heard that Mary was not well and wrote her a note telling her how much pleasure she brought to my life with her music. Her daughter was so moved she wrote me, saying, "Mom was still coherent at the time your note arrived, and as I read it to her, it brought a smile to her face." She went on to say that after Mary's death, she had the minister read it at the memorial service. I love classical piano, and four years of living in that house was not enough for me, but Heinzel wanted to retire to Palm Springs.

He wanted to learn to play golf. He had a membership at the Riviera Country Club as well as the yacht club and the Los Angeles Athletic Club. He had taken three lessons from the golf pro at the Riviera when he asked him if he thought he was ready to accept an invitation to play in a tournament. I would have loved to have seen the look on that pro's face. Three lessons and play in a tournament? We enjoyed the Friday night seafood buffet at the Riviera and the Sunday brunch at the yacht club. The elegance of these places made you feel like a celebrity even if you were not one.

The selling feature for moving to Palm Springs was that in the summer, we would rent a place for three months, and that way, we would get to know this country. It sounded good to me. Heinzel was afraid of retirement after being told by many that he was not the type to retire, so we bought a small place on Birdie Way Drive looking up at Bob Hope's place on the hill. It was close to the munic-ipal golf course, and we enjoyed hacking our way around a couple of times a week. It was a cute lit-tle two bedroom with two baths with a pool in the backyard. It was very private, and although I never learned to swim, I enjoyed the pool. The think-ing was, if he liked retirement, we would sell both places and find one to our liking. Being close to the municipal golf course, it would mean a quick sale if he did not like being retired, and we would move back to Pacific Palisades.

We were always going somewhere and doing something. I thought it was the nature of a Pisces person to come up with creative ideas of places to go, but now that I know myself better, it was the joy that he was bringing to me, and my happiness gave him pleasure.

It was spring, and the tree in our backyard was blooming; they looked like limes to me. I thought, *Let's get some vodka and make vodka tonics.* The limes kept growing and became grapefruit. How do you tell a grapefruit tree from a lime tree when you have grown up in Maryland?

We talked a lot; we sat for hours talking. Heinzel told me about his parents, that he had found a yarmulke in his father's dresser drawer one time, and his grandmother had a chicken in the pot every Sunday. They never claimed any Jewish faith. He asked me to make matzo ball soup for him, and I got pretty good at it.

Elizabeth
Looking for Love

Happiness is contagious; you can spread it, and I can help! It took me so long to find happiness—forty-seven years to be exact. Why? Because I didn't know how. I was like so many young people today; it came in spurts. A new dress, a new house, or a compliment, and you have a moment of happiness.

I lacked confidence in myself; I felt I was ugly because my front teeth protruded. There was no way I was going to get braces, so I worked on them myself. Each night before going to sleep, I leaned over and pushed my teeth into the board holding the mattress until it hurt. My thinking was if I did this at night and was not eating, my teeth would reset themselves.

Praise is important in a child's life, and I never received any from anyone. I craved love. I knew my grandparents loved me, but I needed more than just knowing it. I needed to be hugged and praised. Starved for love, I married the first person who asked me; I wanted to be a part of something or someone. Everyone I knew was getting married. I had a strong desire to have a child, something to love, and it was not happening. Nine months went by, and I went to see a doctor to find out what was wrong. Nothing was wrong, and the next month, I was pregnant.

My husband was a good man, but he was not what I was looking for in a husband. He was from a broken home and needed love too. After a few years, I got up the nerve to tell him I wanted out of the marriage; I was not happy. What I did not say, because I didn't want to hurt him, was that I was looking for love and I was not getting it from him. I married him to be getting married; I never felt love. I was not sure what it felt like to be "in" love.

My definition of love is "The desire to do with and for without expecting anything in return."

I had been looking for a feeling, one of excitement at the sight of a special someone, and mad, passionate sex like you see in the movies. I am a Scorpio, and we are known to be sexual people, but so far, this had escaped me.

I remember asking a fellow employee if he was "in love" because he seemed so happy, more so than usual, and he told me, "No, I am not in love. In heat, maybe, but not in love." I had never heard that before; I thought being in heat was for animals. I fell silent, not knowing how to respond to a statement like that.

Germans have a reputation for being cold and lacking sexual experience, unlike what we hear about the French. Maybe I was looking in the wrong country for a mate! When Heinzel told me Ursula hated sex, I should have known why. Her response to him was, "OK, but get it over with as soon as possible." Even though his marriage was one of convenience, he was a good husband and father. He said after the war, life was different. He had broken his arm in the service, and Ursula was a nurse and had taken care of him. She was the only women he knew, and she was in a lost state at that time too. She asked him to marry her.

I married him because I knew he was the answer to my prayers. God sent him to me, or me to him. We were married in Las Vegas by the justice of the peace; my son, Tom, and his girlfriend stood up for us. After the wedding, the four of us went to see the Siegfried and Roy show. This was the best show in town; they had two beautiful big white tigers they had trained. Now, if life is just a bowl of cherries, I need to find that bowl.

Heinzel smoked like a train and drank like a fish. He smoked most of his life even when he was in the service, so that had been a long time. I smoked for many years, too, but had given it up for several years by then. His drinking started after he lost his son and got worse after he lost his wife. OK, how would I handle this? First things first. Let's work on the smoking. Knowing change has to come from within, I started praying about the smoking. I prayed to God to remove his desire for cigarettes.

An End to Smoking

I'M NOT SURE HOW LONG it took, but he came to me one afternoon, and said, "Schätzchen (my new name, and he told me it was like *darling* in German), I booked us an eleven-day cruise on the Mexican Riviera, and I am going to smoke my last cigarette before the ship leaves the dock." He did just that and never smoked another cigarette. One down and one to go.

Being German and not even drinking beer is special. He had such a dislike for his father, smelling beer on him and listening to him argue with his mother constantly; he never wanted to be like that. His father telling him he wished he had been the one who got killed instead of his brother did not help the situation.

There are ways to get people to do everything. There is a reason for all human behavior and a solution to every problem, and I believe it. Criticizing and complaining will not get the job done. I started telling him how proud I was of him at parties when he didn't drink too much, or I would say, "You are so out of character when you drink too much, and people don't get to know the real you." The next time, I would say, "I am so proud of you when you behave like you did to-night." He wasn't drinking because he liked the taste; he was drinking for the effect of it, so he drank vodka on the rocks. Weekdays were good. He came home to a home-cooked meal of fish, which he loved. Espe, our Mexican housekeeper, kept the house clean and his clothes just as he wanted them.

All that sweet talk about drinking was good, but it was not getting the job done. One Sunday after-noon I went out to work in the garden and taped him in one of his drunken stupors. I was a Mary Kay beauty consultant for a period just prior to go-ing to California and attending seminars in Dallas, Texas; it was suggested that we bring tape record-ers with us to capture what was being taught. All these messages come from God, and this was a re-ally good idea. Thank you, God, for this one.

A HOLY MOMENT

No More Drinking!

HE WAS IN THE GARDEN room on the *L*-shaped sofa, and I just put the tape recorder on the coffee table and went out to play with the flowers. I do not know how long it took him to listen to it, and I never said a word about having recorded him, but one day he came to me and said, "Schatzchen, I listened to that tape you had on the table, and I know that was me because it was definitely my voice"—he had a heavy German accent—"and I am here to tell you I will never drink another drop of alcohol as long as I live." And he didn't. I continued to have my glass of wine with my meals, and he was fine with that.

There are two kinds of drinkers. One type is someone who never drinks on an empty stomach because they don't want to feel it or become inebriated. The other kind drinks just to get drunk, thinking he is going to solve his problems, but he is just making them worse. Heinzel drank vodka on the rocks. He was not drinking because he liked the taste of it; he was drinking solely for the effect. Life got a lot better after that. God gave me a challenge, but he also gave me the solution to handle it.

I also found out you can live happily in a marriage without sex. We were two people who had a strong desire to please each other, and it worked. Heinzel had hypertension and took high blood pressure pills. High-pressure jobs will do that to you. Once you are on them, it is never easy to get off.

Accepting Peter's Death

NEXT, WE WORKED ON THE loss of his son, Peter. Every time he heard the theme from the movie *Doctor Zhivago*, he would yell, "Turn that off; I can't stand it!" Peter was good about calling his parents, and the last time he spoke with Peter, he told him he had just seen the movie *Doctor Zhivago* and how much he loved it. So now he associates the theme with Peter's death. I talked him into changing his thinking, and so when he heard that theme, he should remember all the good things about Peter. I said, "Think of it as God wanting you to remember Peter today."

Selling Pacific Palisades

THE DECISION WAS MADE. IT had been a couple of years now since he retired, and he loved it. All those people who were telling him he would not be happy being retired were wrong. They didn't know he had a playmate and one who wanted to learn to play golf too. It was time to sell the house on Birdie Way, and the real estate market was down. OK, we would rent it out and sell the Pacific Palisades house first. That market moved faster, and it would put an end to our monthly trips in to check on the gardener to be sure all the plants were still living.

To sell a house, you must do a number of things, and one of them is have a termite inspection. I had discovered a white tunnel running up the wall in the garage and mentioned it to Heinzel, thinking it was something that needed looking into. It turned out to be termites, or so we were told. What did we know? We had the house exterminated at that time.

Greed sets in, and people take advantage of those of us trying to sell our homes. Now we were being told this had to be done again because these are different kinds of termites. These termites came from a different country. We needed to tent the house and throw out all the food in the refrigerator, and we could not stay there while this was being done. What's a person to do? You want to sell your house, and you need this certificate of completion. Do termites have birth certificates? How did he know they came from a different country?

You are over a barrel for sure with these people. Even if we had been given a certificate of birth on the prior termites, they were still going to get the job. Returning to the house a few days later, Heinzel went straight to the backyard. I have never seen him work so fast in my life. All the plants had been taken down and were sitting on the small stone wall in the backyard that had been installed many years ago to hold the earth in place. He never was one to do anything in the yard, and to watch him going as fast as he could to get those plants back up was a funny sight to see.

He remembered that the buyer wanted that hanging garden to stay just as it was.

Time marched on, and we finally sold that house. And after a couple of years of renting the house on Birdie Way, we were able to sell it too.

Now, we were living in our new home in Palm Springs—actually, Palm Desert, a short distance east of Palm Springs. It is a country club environment. We were carrying out the plan, learning to play golf. Our community college, the College of the Desert, offered golf lessons, and we took them. Our instructor looked and acted like Lee Trevino, so it made our learning experience fun.

Heinzel was not a physical person, and golf was a challenge for him. Our head pro commented on that fact to me one day, and I had not realized there are people who can watch someone doing something and mimic them, and there are others who cannot. Some people create a mental picture of what they have just seen and do it. I learned to dance doing this. Learning to play golf brought a lot of pleasure to us and enhanced our lives tremendously.

When summer came, we looked for places to rent for the three-month period, and it was always golf related. He saw an ad in the auto club magazine informing everyone about the best-kept secret in all of California: Pacific Grove Golf Course. It was a beautiful course in the Monterey/Carmel area with nine holes on the ocean, and we could walk; we liked walking. I have such fond memories of that course. I loved everything about it.

The driving range was full of deer, and if you happened to hit one, it just moved a little. Some of them rested by the tee box; it was like having a gallery of deer. Such a course—up and down hills, around beautiful homes, and views of the ocean everywhere. After a day on that course, you slept well; you were really tired. All that fresh air and exercise is so healthy. We always went to a nice place for a seafood dinner after golf. The Fisher's Wife in Pacific Grove was a favorite of mine. Palm Desert is not known for its seafood.

The main hazard on that golf course and many in that area is the ice plant. It has pretty little flowers of different colors but is impossible to hit out of. If your ball lands in it, your best bet is to take an unplayable lie. It is full of a sticky substance and looks like a blooming rubber plant. I tried hitting out of it one time, not realizing I was destroying my pants. Once I put the pants in the wash, I noticed that the fluid from the ice plant had turned brown and spotted them.

My first thought was that I had been around

someone who had dropped a plate of food around me and it had splattered all over my pants until I started thinking about where I had worn them last. That was the first summer away from home, and we rented an apartment in Monterey from a schoolteacher.

It was time to decide where we wanted to go again; summer was on the way. I created our ad, and it read, "Retired golfing couple is seeking accommodations for a three-month period, no drinking, no smoking, no pets, and no parties." We were bombarded with calls to rent places. This was a time before computers and cell phones. I called the chamber of commerce to get the name of the newspaper to run the ad. Our first ad was placed in the *Carmel Pine Cone,* and that is where we played golf in Pacific Grove.

One couple wanted us to stay in their place for free. They were leaving town and wanted someone to look after it. We turned them down; Heinzel said we were not for hire and that they wanted to tell us what to do. Summers got to be a lot of fun. I still missed Pacific Palisades and our beautiful home at the ocean, but this was an interesting experience.

The next summer, we rented a place on the Snake River from an old couple. We played unlimited golf all summer at the Canyon Springs Country Club in Twin Falls, Idaho. We walked among the fruit trees and picked and ate all we wanted. The groundskeepers were so nice and told us they didn't spray the trees, so we could eat all we wanted without chemical concern.

We saw our first fish farm and ate a lot of flounder that summer. We also enjoyed living on the river, watching the water-skiers and boaters.

The following summer we rented a big house with a five-car garage in Carson City, Nevada. We only used a small portion of this house—the den, bedroom, kitchen, and bath. It had a very large living room with a baby grand piano, a dining room, upstairs bedrooms, and a balcony off the master suite.

A Visit from a Frog

ONE MORNING AS I STOOD in front of the mirror in the bathroom, I had the strongest urge to lift the lid on the tank of the toilet; it was functioning fine—no problem with it—but the urge was so great, I gave in. Oh my goodness! A little black frog was sitting there on the rod, and he just looked at me; he never moved or tried to jump. How did you get in there, little frog? An immediate request went to Heinzel: "Get a bucket, and come help me rescue this precious frog!" I encouraged him to jump in the bucket, and Heinzel took him outside. The question still lingers in my mind. Did God ask me to rescue that little frog, or did that frog send me a mental message that he needed to be rescued?

We played three different courses in that area. The owners of that home had purchased the property with a five-car garage and a cement slab where a house had been. They were going to England for the summer to visit his family and wanted someone in their home in case of fire again.

On weekends we drove all around, sightseeing and getting to know the place. We left the courses to the working people those days. Our golf was not that great, and we liked to take our time; it was still a learning process.

Several weekends, we drove up the Kingsbury Grade to Tahoe. We had Sunday brunch at Harrah's, looking out over the whole area, and after brunch, we played the craps tables. Another Sunday, we drove to Graeagle to the Plumas Pines Golf Course, a bit of heaven on earth if there ever was one in the Sierra Nevada Mountains.

The following summer we went to Scotland, rented clubs, and spent most of our time playing the municipal golf course in Troon, staying in bed-and-breakfasts. It had three levels of difficulty: one for good golfers, one for kids, and one for mediocre golfers—that was us. After golf, we went to the big clubhouse for lunch. This clubhouse was friendly and welcoming.

We made the mistake of going into a men's club, and I was approached immediately and asked if I knew where I was. I thought I was just in a clubhouse, but they have men's and women's clubs over there, and I was asked to leave.

That was a great summer; we were all over Scotland and England. One day while playing a different course, we only got to play five holes. We were following a foursome of men and were not aware of the gorse bushes and how they eat golf balls. We stopped playing and were trying to stay a comfortable distance back so as not to bother them, and one of them approached us and asked if we would like to play through. At times like this, I am the mouthpiece. "This is so embarrassing," I said. "We have lost all our golf balls, and we don't know how to get back to the starter, so we are following you."

"Oh, my dear," he said, "would you like some golf balls?"

"Thank you so much, but I'm afraid we will just lose your balls too." We decided to give up for the day.

On one course we played, the starter had to let us know when the green was clear. He looked through a spyglass of some kind. The first green was about fifty feet up from the tee box. Talk about scary! Here we are, just trying to hit the ball straight, and now we have to hit it up in the air. How do you do that?

Got to see Turnberry Country club, which is owned by President Trump now. Halfway House Restaurant across the road provides a lively, intimate setting for those out on the course, and you would think you were in the United States with all the pictures of Arnold Palmer hanging everywhere.

TIME FOR SURGERY

We then went back home, and it was time for a yearly physical. Heinzel was told he had a hernia on his aorta, which is the main blood supply, and if left unattended, it could rupture, leaving him with only a half hour of life unless caught immediately. This was the message he received from his doctor. This message came from his general practitioner, so surgery was scheduled and performed very successfully by Dr. Hurad, a specialist in that field.

Feeling good about having this behind us, we decided to go to Las Vegas and celebrate. We loved playing the craps table at Binion's Horseshoe—it was our favorite casino with ten times odds—and stayed across the street at the Four Queens Hotel.

Being away from home, Heinzel evidently took his medication twice. During the night, he got up to go to the bathroom and fell to the floor. You don't think a six-foot-two, 180-pound person is heavy unless you are trying to pick him up from the floor. I managed to get him in the bathroom and on the toilet. He hit his head on something, I'm not sure what; now blood was everywhere, and he lost control of his bowels. This is when your marriage vows kick in: for better or worse.

I steadied him on the toilet and commanded him not to move while I called for help. "Operator, I have an emergency in this room and need help." Three burly men arrived at the door within minutes. I was still in my nightgown. Who cared?

Not wanting to be taken in the ambulance in this condition, he asked me to clean him up a bit. Once he was in the hands of the men, I slipped back into the bedroom and put some clothes on, gathered his medicine, and we were off to the University Medical Center, where he spent the next eleven days in the trauma center of the hospital. The doctor who met me assured me that he was going to be fine. "Whatever he has, we can fix it" were his words.

The next morning was a different story. The doctor informed me that all his vital signs were shutting down, and they were going to try to save him. To do this, they put him in an induced coma. I could see him for ten minutes every two hours. Now I waited all day in a little eight-by-twelve room furnished with comfortable chairs, not wanting to lose my parking space by going back to the hotel. Now I was meeting new people coming in all day for different reasons. Families gathered to make decisions about loved ones, to keep them alive or let them go, to harvest their organs or not.

One young woman was having her tonsils removed and experienced a brain aneurism; her family was told she was brain-dead. These were tough decisions to make—many sad stories and many people needing comfort.

A Free Room

AFTER BEING THERE FOR A few days, I found out there was a room available in the Ronald McDonald House. There were no children in the hospital at that time, and I could have the room.

Now I was living at the hospital. I could park my car and walk over to the waiting room. What a blessing! Before, I had to drive around and around looking for a parking place.

Visiting hours in this particular area were ten minutes every two hours. When I arrived in the waiting room, I signed in and waited for two hours, put on protective gear, then went and saw my husband lying there like a dead person. After a week, I decided to start talking to him, telling him to breathe on his own so we could get out of here. The sooner he could breathe on his own, the sooner we could go home. The nurse heard me saying these words and commented, "You are doing the right thing."

On day eleven, I decided I must do something. I must find a church and talk to God. I could not keep sitting there forever. It was a tough decision because I had a great parking place and hesitated to move my car because I would have trouble finding a spot as good as that one again, but the only way to find a church was by car.

I Gave Heinzel to God

SITTING IN MY CAR, I asked God to help me find a church. I headed out, turned right, and drove two blocks, and a beautiful church appeared before me. It was open. I went in and had a chat with God.

God, it's me, Elizabeth, and we need to talk. My husband, Heinzel, has been in intensive care now for eleven days. I've been sitting here in this waiting room for eleven days to be exact, and I want to go home. I put my husband, Heinzel, before you, and if you want him, please take him now. I cannot keep doing this, but if you do not want him, please give him back to me so we can go home.

A Heavenly Surprise

THE NEXT MORNING AS I arrived for my visit, I could not believe my eyes. There he was, sitting up in bed with a nurse standing beside him! His first words were, "Schätzchen, where have you been?" He was moved to a room with another man and remained there for three days before we were allowed to leave for home.

That was so special. Now I could talk with him and his roommate too. I got the nurse for them and got them water. I was assisting the nursing staff.

It was like being born again, and his roommate asked, "Where did you find that woman?"

Going Home

IT WAS TIME TO LEAVE for home, and Heinzel said to me, "Schätzchen, I think we should stay another day or two because I don't feel like I can help you with the driving."

He was not to worry. I was happy to do it all by myself, and it was only a four-hour drive from Las Vegas to Palm Desert.

Life got good again. I appreciated how good it could be now that I had gotten to see the other side. The more we appreciate, the more God gives us to appreciate. I am so grateful for what I have now and what I have had.

I've been so many beautiful places, traveled the world, met so many wonderful people, and learned so much about life and how to live it.

We were home now, and it had never looked so good. The sun was shining, the birds were singing, and the mountains had never been more beautiful. The golf course had been waiting for us. Heinzel was told by the doctors at the trauma center to check in with his primary care physician in a couple of weeks, which he did.

Everything was back to normal. We were playing golf (if that is what you can call his game; I call it more goof than golf, but he enjoys it, so who cares?). I was constantly reminding him to keep it in the fairway.

His doctor had him come back again in a couple of weeks, and this time, he doubled the strength of his blood pressure medication. When he asked why, he was told, "You can handle it." Well, it turned out he could not handle it.

He was puffing up like a frog, and a sticky, watery substance was coming out of his nose. Always concerned about his weight, he asked me to make a cucumber dish with onions and vinegar for him. He was not gaining weight. Something else was going on, and I called the doctor to inform him.

Doctors return calls at the end of the day evidently because we waited for hours with no call. He was watching the Clarence Thomas hearings on the television in the den and called to me in the kitchen to say he was going back to the bedroom to lie down.

"OK, we are still waiting for the doctor to return our call, and I will come back there in a few minutes and check on you" was my reply.

Oh my God, my God, he was dead! He was blue, really blue. I had never seen a blue person before. I called 911, and big fire trucks arrived. Not knowing what else to do, I was standing at the garage door to be sure they found our place.

They took him out of the bed, placed him on the floor, and opened his neck; blood started flowing on the white carpet now, and I was thinking he had been dead for some time now; what would he be like if they brought him back to life? They were still pressing his chest as they took him to the ambulance. The doctor who had performed the surgery on the aorta met me in the little room they use for conferences in the emergency room, but his general practitioner never showed his face.

I had been alone now for a couple of days and was stressed to the max. He had paid all our bills. I didn't know how much money we had, how much we owed, or whether I could remain living in our home and continue to meet our financial obligations.

As I was getting out of bed one morning, my legs gave way, and I fell to the floor. I called 911 and was taken to the hospital.

Having been a volunteer at this hospital, I was given a special room and treated royally. I remember the sign reading VIP—very important person. Three days later a friend brought me home and suggested I return to Maryland to family, so I called my son in West Virginia and paid him a visit. I remember sitting on the floor with my back against the front of his bed, watching a special golf tournament.

Golf got me through the next few years. I played, I watched, I practiced, or I recorded the Dinah Shore, Frank Sinatra, and Don Drysdale tournaments. On Christmas Day, I was out playing golf by myself, and a friend saw me and sent her husband out to join me. Some friends make your day; a real friend makes your life.

My friend and neighbor Ellie Piers has a son named Robbie who comes to visit her and likes to play golf, so she calls me when he is coming for a visit, saying, "Robbie is coming for a visit and would like to play golf with you. Would you set up some times and play with him?" After one of our games, I was invited for dinner later in the evening. Sitting at the table, Ellie told Rob that I was having a problem with stress. Robbie is a psychiatrist in San Francisco, and he asked me if I knew what stress was.

I had never given thought to what it is; I just know what it does to me. So I told him, "I don't know how to answer that."

"Stress," he told me, "is fear of the unknown."

Holy mackerel! That was exactly what my problem was. I was afraid I could not continue to live there, and I didn't know what to do.

Peace Comes in the Form of a Ledger

I LEFT AFTER DINNER AND could not wait for the Office Depot to open in the morning to purchase a large ledger for my desk. I wrote on the top-left side my monthly income, and down the side I listed my financial obligations, grouping them as utilities, taxes, et cetera. After that, I was fine. Being able to see them and recording them each month made a big difference.

As I sit here thinking about that marriage and how I grew from it, I am so grateful God was directing my path all the way. What a guy you sent me to, God. He was a pilot in the German Air Force. He knew he could never kill another human being and had to become a pilot. As he told me, no one knows what you are doing up there.

Later in life, he became a close friend of Jimmy Roosevelt's. Who would have thought that? The son of President Roosevelt becoming a friend of one of Hitler's pilots. God was with this guy every step of the way.

Saved by Two Russian Sailors

WE WERE ON A CRUISE. We stopped in Istanbul for shopping, five hundred shops under one roof. Some of these shops were the size of a closet, but they were still considered a shop.

I saw a leather shop I wanted to explore just outside the entrance with large glass windows. There was a beautiful full-length white leather coat with black piping. We were encouraged to dicker for the price, and we must have dickered too long because we could see the gangplank of our ship being taken up, and we were two blocks from it.

These ships have to pay a docking fee and need to leave on time. This particular time, the ship could not get in close to the shops because there were too many ships at that time.

With our passports on the ship and not knowing where our next port was, Heinzel panicked and decided to walk his fingers around the wall of the harbor to shorten the distance and hold the ship until I could walk the distance to get there.

In his effort to do so, his fingers gave way, and he slid down the wall into the oily black harbor water, skinning his face on the wall as he went down. I was standing there with my beautiful coat in a bag, and I started yelling, "Help!" in the very loudest voice I could muster, and the cruise ship heard me. *A holy moment!* More important than that, two Russian sailors on the ship docked there in the harbor jumped in that nasty water to help him out. He had blood on his face, and he was covered in black oil.

He had ingested some of that water and became very sick in a couple of days. We were due to arrive in Washington, DC, in two weeks. He was committed to a job for President Ronald Reagan to investigate small business loans. Working with Donald Regan, he said he felt very special, walking the halls and having people call out to him, "Good morning, Mr. Secretary," thinking he was Donald Regan. They looked a lot alike.

I loved that period of my life, being put up in a darling apartment hotel in Georgetown, walking the streets of DC. The Mall had never been so beautiful. We went to Clyde's for lunch, and I worked on the Inaugural Committee with the Sinatra Group. It was a very cold winter, and being from California, we didn't have the proper attire for that weather.

We were invited to every ball but did not attend because it was too cold. We arrived in October of 1984 and returned home in January of 1985.

He is in heaven. I know this for sure; he told me he was going there. "Schätzchen, if there is a heaven, I'm going there." Oh, how do you know that was my question? Because I can say in all honesty, I have never done anything to hurt another human being in my entire life.

A more peaceful death could not be possible. He never made a sound. The house was completely quiet, and I never heard a peep out of him.

You never said, I'm leaving
You never said goodbye.
You were gone before we knew it
And only God knows why.
In life I loved you dearly
In death I love you still.
In my heart I hold a place
That only you can fill.
It broke my heart to lose you
But you didn't go alone.
A part of me went with you
The day God took you home.

—AUTHOR UNKNOWN

He was the best thing that ever happened to me. He was so full of confidence, married to a woman ten years younger than himself without a jealous bone in his body. He was always wanting to do something for me, giving me a face-lift or a trip or taking me shopping for clothes.

One day the telephone rang, and we were both in the kitchen, and it was a man calling. His wife had died, and he had asked my brother for my number, thinking we could start a relationship. Hearing me say, "You know I am married now" when I hung up the telephone, he asked who that was. I told him who it was, and I loved his response: "Schätzchen, as long as there is breath in this body, you are mine." And so it was till death did us part.

Special people never die; they live in our hearts forever.

Those we love don't go away,
they walk beside us every day…
unseen, unheard but always near;
still loved, still missed,
and very dear.

—AUTHOR UNKNOWN

As I look back on my life, I communicated with Heinzel more that anyone. Knowing I was not an educated person, he made me feel so special, and I never forgot the day he said, "Schätzchen, you are not an educated person, but you are very intelligent, and by the time I finish with you, you will have the equivalent of a college education."

That comment started my educational journey. I put myself through finishing school because I wanted to know how to set a proper table, how to greet people, and what to say, when to say it, and how to say it. I wanted him to be proud of me.

I had to be careful what I said because he had such a desire to please me; he would make it happen. We watched the British Open on the television, and I commented about how I would love to be there to watch Greg Norman. The next thing I knew, we were in Turnberry, Scotland, eating in the little restaurant across from the hotel; you would think you were in America with all the pictures on the wall of Arnold Palmer.

Life goes on, and I was out there talking to God again because, as I said a long time ago, he is the only one who knows the kind of man I can get along with. We talk a lot more when I am single. I don't know where these things come from, but they arrive.

Whispers from God—everyone must have them; they are just so busy they ignore them. Each night before going to bed, I go to my dining room window, look up at the sky, and see a star. For some reason I heard or read, if it is sparkling, you should talk to it; it is your direct passage to God. If I arrive and it is not there, I stand there, and it arrives. At this same window, I became aware there were three palm trees, and the one in the middle was the tallest.

God has a way of letting me know he is there with me. Looking down to the ground, I could not believe it, but there was a cross created from two palm fronds.

I was working for IBM in Washington, DC, stressed to the max. I was dating a very bright, very tall, handsome man, just the kind of man I always wanted to be married to. I was not aware of and had never heard the terms "manic depressive" or "bipolar" until I experienced it. This is a man who can function as a normal human being and, just like lightning, can change.

He started accusing me of doing all kinds of things.

If he tells you he has installed infrared lights in your home and sees your every move, don't even try to defend yourself. When this is happening, it will be a waste of your time. I have never been so frightened by someone in my life. A Jekyll and Hyde. How would I get out of this situation?

Hello, Saint Martha

IT WAS LUNCHTIME. I WAS at work and decided to find a church.

The Cathedral of St. Matthew was two blocks up the street. This is the church where President Kennedy's service was held. As I entered, I was drawn to the candles, and there it was: a novena to Saint Martha: "Light your candle, and within nine Tuesdays, Saint Martha will honor your request." I must have come across as desperate because she answered my request right away. I received a call from him within days saying he had met someone new and would not be seeing me any longer. Whew! What a gal, this Saint Martha. This was the first time she came to my rescue but not the last.

A Response to My Prayer Card

IN MONTEREY, CALIFORNIA, ON A Tuesday, feeling the desire to talk to Saint Martha, I struck out to find a church. Having written to Pope Francis, I wanted to know if he had received my letter. I asked God to let me know by putting a feather in my path. As I was entering the church, a young man with a yellow tank strapped to his back was leaving, and it turned out to have been a vacuum cleaner. I always head to the front of the church, wanting to get the full impact of it, and kneeling there, I saw a little white object on the floor to the left in front of me. Was that a feather? How did that feather escape the vacuum cleaner? There it was: a little white feather.

Looking for a place to park my vehicle before going into a restaurant, I saw that the lot was full.

It was an ideal spot to park, and after talking with the couple doing the ticketing and giving them one of my prayer cards, they allowed me to park in a spot free. Walking to the restaurant, I saw another feather there in front of me. I now had enough feathers to create my own bird.

This prayer card has brought so much happiness to my life. It came to me one morning after meditating, and I started out writing it on three-by-five-inch cards until a friend recommended I get Vistaprint to print it out for me:

> Thank you, God, for taking over my
> life, directing my path, and using
> me to bring happiness to others.
> I am receiving now.

A little old lady seated herself beside me in church one morning and commented, "I think I am late for this service," and I agreed but told her she was early for the next one. I gave her a prayer card, and she read it, as everyone does. Then she looked me in the eye and said, "You have no idea how much I need this right now." I did not expect that, coming from someone her age.

An old waiter came close to me one night in an upscale restaurant, and I gave him one of my prayer cards. He read it, looked me in the eye, and said, "You have no idea how much I need this right now. I lost the love of my life this morning, and I had to come to work tonight."

The priest asked us to be generous to the young man as we were leaving church that morning since he was going off to study to become a priest. I never take extra money with me, and as I was leaving, I apologized for not having money, but I gave him a prayer card. He read it, looked at me, and said, "This is better than money." *Wow!* Who would have thought a young person would ever say something is better than money? It made my day!

Lonely and alone again, now for three years, I took up my conversation with God about sending me someone and the fact he is the only one who knows the kind of man I can get along with. We walked and talked around our complex at Chaparral Country Club. Friends asked if they could walk with me, and I would tell them, "This is my time with God."

Arrived on My Computer Screen

IT HAD BEEN MY THOUGHT that I needed to be outside for God to hear me, free from the many layers of insulation used to control the temperature in the house. My computer is a MacBook Air, and I think the "Air" part is that God is in it. I always wondered if I had to be outside for God to hear my thoughts, and one day when I arrived at the computer, I saw a thought going through a rock, and it was a very large rock. Now I know that no amount of insulation in my attic keeps my thoughts from being received. As I talk with God, I know he hears me; whether I am inside or outside, he sends me a message letting me know it.

I am God's boots on the ground. I ask him to put people in my path, and I will do everything in my power to help them. My thinking is, "Always leave them better than I find them. Listen, and never try to top their stories with one I think is better."

God Answers All My Prayers Frederick—A New Husband

THE CALL CAME FROM A friend, Rolla; I had been helping with her golf game. It was New Year's Day, 1994. God uses everyone. "Would you like to play golf with us today?" *Us* meant Rolla, her husband, Frank, and his brother Fred, who was here visiting for a few days. She went on to say, "Maybe the two of us could ride together in your cart and let the boys ride in our cart."

A *holy moment* for sure.

As I look back, so many holy moments have happened to me since that day on Mimosa Lane when I called out to God for help. Tears were flowing like a swollen river. It felt good to cry, and I had a good cry for sure.

Wanting to sell my home, I knew that things needed to be removed to make it more appealing to a buyer. The mattress that I wanted taken to the trash was removed by a man who showed up at my door saying, "I understand you have a mattress you want taken to the trash." Where did he come from?

Several people responded to an ad for a free refrigerator in the basement and removed it, which was not an easy chore. It had to be taken up six steps and pushed up a hill.

When I see an old woman working as a waitress, I say to myself, "There but for the love of God, go I." From the day I married Heinzel, I never worked another day in my life. I volunteered but never received a paycheck.

My plan was to help my cousin Pat relocate to California, return to Maryland, buy a small townhouse on a river, and find a job. My remaining furniture was in storage waiting for me.

God had a different plan. Little did I know that Fred was the same kind of man I had been married to: a banker. After our golf game, Fred wanted to be with me every minute he was here. We walked El Paseo one evening, in and out of the art galleries; he came over for salad, rolls, and wine. We talked about our past lives, wives, and husbands, and how painful it is to make a mistake and how important it is to know what you want.

It was time for him to return home to Smyrna, North Carolina, where he retired from working as the executive vice president of the Federal Reserve of New York. I would go back to practicing my golf and volunteering at Eisenhower Medical Center. After he returned home, I was talking with his sister-in-law, Rolla. She told me he was a doctor, and I wanted to know what kind of doctor he was. She said he had a PhD in economics. When I learned this, my thought was, *Oh, God, these bankers are getting bigger.*

We wrote letters and talked on the telephone occasionally. It was expensive to make calls out of state in those days. Meanwhile, he stayed busy, being asked to travel all over the world on business by the Federal Reserve, and it was a good thing because it was a mistake for him, a single man, to buy a home back on a dirt road, even though it was a beautiful property on a bay, with a large porch down one side of it. It was nicely landscaped with a circular drive in the front and a sunken birdbath in a grassy area, but it was still a lonely place for a single man to live.

There was a very large osprey nest in one of the trees on his property, and I had never seen an osprey before or even heard of one. Watching them fly out over the bay, you see why they are called an osprey.

I was spending my time at the driving range practicing golf. If I wasn't playing, I was practicing or volunteering as a walking scorekeeper for the LPGA Nabisco, which used to be known as the Dinah Shore. I also scored for the Sinatra celebrity tournament, Don Drysdale's tournament, and occasionally the qualifying PGA Tour. Scoring for the Don Drysdale and Sinatra tournaments, I got to ride in the cart with them.

Fred loved North Carolina; he had vacationed there many years with his son Geoffrey. It was the middle of March and time for our club championship, which I had won the year before, and I would now be defending my title.

Rolla informed Fred that she and Frank would be out of town for a week, and maybe he would like to come back, stay in their home, and be here to support me while I was defending my championship. It was a happy thought for him and a disaster for me. They both were for this relationship developing. Frank was either looking out for his brother because he had been alone so long or wanted to be able to spend time with him in their retirement years.

Fred arrived before my game and wished me

luck; he also watched us tee off on the first tee. It isn't easy defending to begin with, and knowing you have a new suitor out there watching you makes it even tougher to concentrate. I lost the championship but gained a new husband.

The following Sunday we played golf with a nice couple from Canada. Fred said I embarrassed him when I introduced myself and said I was "husband hunting" and he was a prospect, but I know he loved it. We had been spending so much time together that I told him (while making dinner) I was beginning to feel married. I could tell he liked the thought.

He does have a sense of humor. He teased me about dinner being hot dogs, and it was sole and a lovely dinner. I could tell he really cared for me and was showing signs of wanting a physical relationship, which I had no desire for at that time.

He shared his thoughts with me one night on what he was thinking while still in North Carolina, and it had to do with sex. He wondered if I would engage in a sexual encounter because he saw me as "prim." This was not the first time I had heard this. When I married the first time, I was working for the telephone company, and one of the young women working with me said, "You don't look like you would ever do anything like that." I'm not sure what that look is, but I guess I have it.

He had been single for many years, and this was important to him, and I understood it. We met in January, and now he was back in March. We were golfing, cooking for each other, walking at the street fair, and doing little things together. One night, he arrived and asked if we could talk.

And the question was, "Will you marry me?"

I almost fell off my own sofa. Shocked, I sat quietly for a minute or so; then I told him, "I think I can make you very happy."

His response was "I know you can."

After he shared this information with his son, Geoffrey, his remark was, "Dad, what's the hurry?" His answer was that the hurry was he had finally found someone he wanted to marry. Rolla and Frank were very supportive of this relationship; she insisted on taking me shopping for a wedding dress and having Frank pay for it. We found a beautiful dress for seven hundred dollars and had it sent to Fred's home, which saved paying California taxes.

Should we go to Las Vegas and get married by the justice of the peace like Heinzel and I did? "No way" was the answer to that idea. I wanted to be married by a minister in a church. OK, you make the arrangements, and I will show up. And that is exactly what happened.

A Honeymoon in Charleston, South Carolina

WE WERE MARRIED IN MAY; we put Fred's house up for sale and traveled to Charleston, South Carolina, for our honeymoon. Fred arranged everything. He had seen an ad in the New York Times travel section about a bed-and-breakfast that was out of this world. He booked it for us, and we loved it.

Once we arrived in Palm Desert, Rolla and Frank had a wedding reception for us at Mission Hills Country Club, a beautiful affair with one of the Marx brothers playing the piano.

When the new address labels arrived for the first time, I think from a contribution to St. Jude's hospital, "Dr. & Mrs. Frederick Schadrack," my first thought was, *OK, girl, you have finally made it. Who would have thought this possible? All your life you wanted to marry someone special, and it has finally come about.*

The first year of any marriage is not easy, and this one was no exception. Possessiveness set in and showed its ugly face. We were living in my home where everyone knows me. I am a friendly person; I speak to everyone. I was raised that way. My second sense told me something was bothering him, so I asked, "Is there a problem?"

"Yes, do you have to speak to everyone?"

I had spoken to all the men at the driving range. These men have known me for years; they are the husbands of my friends. If I don't speak to them, they would wonder what was wrong. "Do you think these men are going to leave their wives of fifty plus years for me? I never dated anyone living here, and I married you."

It is important that one must stand their ground, especially in the beginning, and I stood mine—that is, if you want to resolve these problems from the start. "I cannot live that way" was my message to him.

My grandmother taught me that it does not cost anything to speak to another. Years prior to my marriage to Heinzel, I was dating a man who had the same problem with me. One day he asked me if I had to speak to everybody. Then he followed it up with, "You would probably speak to the garbage man; do you think the queen of England would speak to the garbage man?" Wow, he was putting me on the same plane with the queen!

In my distress, I called upon the Lord, and he heard my voice.

Off to Buenos Aires, Argentina

FRED WAS BEING ASKED BY the president of the Federal Reserve to travel to different countries and give his opinion and solutions to boost their economy. The first trip after our marriage was to Buenos Aires, Argentina, and I got to go along.

We arrived on a Friday morning, and Fred's driver met us at the airport and delivered us to our apartment where we thought we would sleep into the next day since it had been an all-night flight. We don't sleep well while flying, and during the flight we hit an air pocket, which caused the plane to drop, it seemed, about ten thousand feet. That kept us awake for sure; was there more to come?

Fred made some phone calls, thinking he would start working Monday, only to find out Paul

Volcker had arrived the same day, and the two of them were to dine with the minister of finance. They met again on Saturday at the minister's home.

How special is this? I thought it was going to look like Mexico; it looked like Paris. There were flower stands and newsstands everywhere. I don't think anyone gets home delivery here in this city, and these people read a lot. Magazines cost between $8.00 and $9.50 for English-speaking people.

All streets were one way and seemed to work very well. There were lots of buses and cabs. I counted forty cabs on Santa Fe street at one time. Trash was put in large bags at the curb every night, and the trash truck ran all night picking it up.

Horns blow all night, and motorcycles are very loud. The dinner hour starts at eight. Most people arrive at nine and as late as ten to start dinner.

There is definitely no statement to be made as far as cars are concerned. Everyone has a small French car of one kind or other, and they all look the same. These people are walking and talking on the telephone all the time. Fred said, "Their phone system is so bad, they all have cell phones." This was 1994, and we didn't have them at home yet that I was aware of.

I got to watch the golf tournaments on the television but could not understand the commentary. The only things I understood were "excellent" and "*perfecto.*"

We were there for four weeks, and I loved every minute of it. I loved being treated like royalty when we went out to dinner. You arrive at the restaurant, and there is a full-size cow on wheels. You are greeted and asked, "Where would you like to sit?" You may sit there all night if you would like. Someone comes to cover your garment if you have placed it on the chair; this is to be sure nothing gets spilled on it. The best beef in the world, and beautiful leather shoes; too bad I cannot wear them because I wear 11 narrow, and they don't make that size.

Our apartment was precious: a living room, bedroom, and bath with a Pullman kitchen. I like to cook, so I found out where the store was and headed out. It was a beautiful store, but my problem was that I don't speak Spanish or read it. It was shopping by sight, and that didn't always work. At first, I thought we would have a carrot salad to go along with some little thing I had purchased in one of the little restaurants.

It was something easy; I bought some raisins and put it together. The next thing, I heard funny sounds coming from Fred's mouth. It sounded like he was eating sticks. The raisins had large seeds in them. What on earth can you do with raisins with seeds in them?

I loved the little restaurants, and I mean really little restaurants, the size of a closet with an ice cream table and two chairs. They do the cooking at home and bring it to the restaurant the next day and sell it. It was very interesting food with nice people too. They show it in the front window, and you go in and buy it to take home or sit and eat it there.

I'm a walker, and I love walking to the park and sitting there people watching most of the time, but occasionally someone would sit down beside me who spoke English. Fred and I met each day for lunch. Two people trying to order lunch in a Spanish-speaking country was a challenge for both of us, but we never went hungry.

We got home, and the first thing Fred wanted to do was play golf. "Me too; let's go." We got to the first tee and found out I could not make a swing. I could not turn my shoulder; it was frozen. My arm would not go any higher than my waist. The problem is when you don't use something, all the little muscles in there come together and try to fix it by tightening up. Given what I know now, if that ever happens again, I will take a club and swing it a little bit each day until it goes away and forget the therapy.

We spent the month of June in Argentina, and the summer months were coming on fast in Palm Desert. It was too hot to stay, and Fred decided he would like to spend the summer in Canada on the West Coast in the Calgary area. On the way, we stopped in Oregon. He played Black Butte Golf course, and I walked with him and the other couple. The next stop was Banff; I had always wanted to visit that place ever since I saw an ad in a magazine. It was so beautiful, like a medieval castle, and Fred played golf on that course too. My arm had to be in very bad condition for me to pass up playing on both of those courses.

Our next stop was Whistler for a week. Wow, how beautiful that is! There were large baskets of flowers hanging everywhere, down every street. They were so beautiful cascading out of their containers.

This was a great summer—seeing places I had never heard of and moving from chalet to chalet and walking in forests, which is one of my favorite things to do. We sat on the little porches built in front of the chalets. It is amazing how comfortable you can be in such a small space. Living in the outdoors is one of my favorite things to do, going to town for breakfast and eating blueberries. They have the biggest blueberries in the world. We had a summer of togetherness that was so peaceful. It was just what we needed—him after working and me just getting to know him better.

Fred was impressed with my cleanliness and that we always left the chalets cleaner than we found them. It was almost like he was expecting the owner to come by and knock a few bucks off our rent.

The following summer we spent in Park City, Utah. Several of our friends had been going there for a number of years. It was my first time to join them since Heinzel and I had always run our own ad, and he was not one to join others or participate in large gatherings. All he wanted or needed was to be with me. After that summer, Fred decided he wanted to know where he was going each year, so we checked out a couple of places close by. We looked at Big Bear Mountain and even went to the San Diego area looking but did not find anything to our suiting.

I remembered a place north of Tahoe that Heinzel and I had visited in the Sierra Nevada Mountains when we were renting the place in Carson City. It was a heavenly sight; once you saw it, you never forgot it. Fred asked me to make a reservation and contact a realtor in the area so we could go for a visit. We arrived and spent three days looking. The realtor gave us keys to five homes for sale or rent. She just let us go in these places by ourselves and look around, and we would get back to her.

When we arrived at 279 Tamarack Court, I fell in love. It was so cozy with a floor-to-ceiling river rock wood-burning fireplace and a big deck across the back and down one side, looking out to the fifteenth green on the Plumas Pines Golf Course and into the Plumas National Forest. There was morning sun on the deck, and it was great for lunch and dinner later in the day.

We made an offer, which was accepted, and now we have a special place to go every summer. What is this "PP" thing going on in my life? I lived in Pacific Palisades with Heinzel, and now I was purchasing a home in Plumas Pines with Fred. It was the perfect place for anyone who likes to hike in the mountains and around lakes, and we both loved it very much.

It was not close to shopping or a hospital. Our grocery store was 1930s-style; it was small with wooden floors and only enough room for one person, but we loved it. It had fresh salad fixings and a great fish and a meat counter.

The Holy Spirit Spoke to Me

THERE WAS A BIG MILLPOND out the back of the store and a great place to hike around the pond with a short path down to the Feather River. This is where the Holy Spirit spoke to me for the first and only time in my life. It's been a couple of years now since Fred passed, and I loved to hike behind the pond, sit at the river, and listen to the water flowing from the mountains over the rocks and into the river, and I got the message: *There is a heart-shaped rock around you.* Oh my gosh, there was one right by my foot.

I was not the same for a couple of days.

Reno is one-hour drive each way, and we made a weekly trip to Costco and had a special lunch somewhere. We were healthy and happy for the first eight years or so.

Winter arrives in September in the mountains, and we never left for Palm Desert until the end of October, so we built a fire in the fireplace every night, it was a two-sided corner fireplace so we could enjoy it in the dining room too.

Living with the Animals

WE LOVED OUR MORNINGS IN Plumas Pines, sitting in the bed on cold winter mornings drinking our coffee, watching the stock market, and seeing the raccoons crossing our yard on their way home to their condo under our neighbor's deck after a night out on the town. This bedroom was the closest thing to sleeping outside. It had two sliding glass doors going out to the deck and two big windows looking out onto the golf course and into the national forest.

One morning I saw a very large raccoon walking ever so slowly across our lawn, and I jumped out of bed and ran to our guest room for a better view of the deck next door to see if she had any signs of trauma, thinking she may have been in a fight with another animal. To my surprise, she had two of the tiniest babies I have ever seen following her. They appeared to be about six inches long. I grabbed the camera to capture a picture of them, but they were so small you could not even see them in the picture.

That mother knew I was at that window, and this window is on the other side of our house. She whipped around so fast, as if to attack me if she needed to. How special to live in an area among wildlife! It was a treat watching the deer eating blueberries from our bush. Our blueberries were very small compared to the ones in Canada but were still tasty.

We normally left the first week of November for our home in the desert, but this year Fred was in treatment for bladder cancer. He had radiation Monday through Friday, and since it was an hour's drive each way, we decided to rent one of the apartments in the hospital. Actually, he was having his head radiated because the cancer was now in his brain. He looked like he was going out to play football when he put on the helmet they created to be sure they only radiated the tumor.

To all our treasured friends:
This is what I know for sure. We went into Reno this afternoon for head measurements, and Fred starts his first radiation on his head tomorrow. It will take three

weeks, at which time we will be back living in the Washoe Medical Center from Monday to Thursday. Friday morning after he gets his radiation, we will head up here for the weekend, where I will light a fire each night in our fireplace and have a wonderful dinner in our dining room. We are making the most of every day in every way we know how.

Our doctor has a very positive attitude and makes us feel that we are going to make it, and we really want to believe him. For those of you who are not aware, Fred has a brain tumor, and it is sitting next to the channel that the fluids run from our brain through our body, and if left as is, it will be fatal very shortly. He has gone through weeks of chemo and radiation at the Washoe Medical Center for bladder cancer this summer, and we thought we were finished with all of this. We lived in the Washoe Medical Center's hotel called the Washoe Inn and were very comfortable. We had a kitchenette, and I was able to cook all our meals, which was a blessing because he did not feel like going out to eat, and it was necessary for him to keep up his weight.

Why do doctors operate on patients who have cancer before killing the cancer cells? Once they go in there as the doctor did, to cut out a large growth sitting under his bladder, he set the cancer cells free to travel throughout his body. They did the same thing to Senator Kennedy. When I heard he had bladder cancer and they were going to remove something, my first thought was "Oh no, they are going to do it again."

Many years ago, my mother had strep throat, and the doctor did not know what to do, so he lanced the blisters in her throat, and the strep germ went into her bloodstream. She died from blood poisoning. They radiate after to keep it from spreading, yet they cut into you and spread it before they operate. I'm not even a doctor, and I know our blood flows throughout our body.

One morning while trying to get out of bed, he slid down to the floor, and I had to call friends to come help him up. That was when the decision was made to head to the desert. This treatment was not working, and he wanted to be back where his family was and much closer to medical treatment.

I called Geoffrey in San Salvador for support, and he was able to meet us in Reno the next morning to help with the drive, which is ten hours. We arrived, and my first thought was, *It's Christmas, and we need a tree;* Fred loved Christmas, and I do too. Geoff helped with the tree and then headed back to his wife, Bonnie, and their daughter, Norah. It was Norah's first Christmas.

I was given the name of a doctor to see when we got to Palm Desert. It was Christmas Eve. Frank, Fred's brother, helped me get him to the doctor's office, and after one look at Fred, the doctor advised me to take him home. He was arranging for hospice and told me to expect them to arrive within hours. What a blessing they are. Thank you, Ronald Reagan, for bringing them to this country. On one of his visits to England, he became aware of hospice service and brought the idea back to the States. Now help is just a phone call away.

Someone came each day, bathed him, and helped meet our needs. Fred only lasted two weeks after we arrived home. Geoffrey and I were both with him when he left for heaven.

"A Love Story" is Fred's memorial service written by Betsy and delivered by Pastor Carl of Hope Lutheran Church. When I married Heinzel, he asked if he could call me Betsy since I represented the American flag to him. Sure, call me anything, but he just introduced me as Betsy to everyone and continued to call me Schatzchen. So I continued to be Betsy to Fred.

Time to Say Goodbye

Saturday as I sat beside Fred and held his hand, I thanked God for answering our prayers. It was the year 1994, and he was living in North Carolina and I living in California, both very lonely people. My prayer was, God, if you only knew how lonely I am, you would send me someone, and you are the only one who knows the kind of person I can get along with. He doesn't have to be rich or handsome, just honest and clean, but someone who needs me.

The same prayer I used for God to send Heinzel to me. If it works, keep using it, right?

After knowing Fred for two months, he proposed marriage, and even though I hardly knew him, I knew God had sent him, so I could not go wrong. I accepted his proposal and told him I would marry him and that I thought I could make him very happy. I believe we harvest what we sow, and I would be very happy too.

In 1994 on New Year's Day at the first tee of Chaparral Country Club, I met Fred for the first time. God used his brother Frank and sister-in-law Rolla to answer our prayers. Fred was so special in so many ways; it would have been a shame for all the people who knew him and loved him to have been deprived of that pleasure.

It was Saturday, and we were home from the hospital for the weekend. We looked forward to going home to our little bit of heaven. I built a rip-roaring fire in the fireplace, and he was sitting on the sofa where he could enjoy it. Radiation had taken its toll on him. As he sat quietly, I asked him to share his thoughts with me, and he said he was repeating the Twenty-Third Psalm. Being familiar with this psalm but wanting to see it in print, I immediately went into the den and printed it out, and as I read it, I was moved by one line especially: "He leads me beside still waters."

Our home in the Sierra Nevada Mountains was a short distance from many lakes, and we loved hiking up the mountains with our lunch in our backpack, sitting on a rock by the water's edge, watching the water lap ever so gently on the shore, and sometimes the wind would blow just enough to make peaks on top of the lake. And when this happened, it looked like the sun was dancing on the water, so sparkly, so beautiful, and so peaceful.

Twelve wonderful years of this, and little did we know God was leading us beside still waters; we thought we were just hiking and having lunch. We took it all in on every hike, all the little wild-flowers up the path, the rocks we related to peo-ple—some very white and beautiful, some brown with mineral lines in them, and some looked old because they had what looked like liver spots on them.

I talked, and he listened about how great it would be if all the young men in the world had a father like him. Geoffrey, Fred's son, was so blessed to have been raised by him.

Fred was a very quiet, private person, and yet he was loved by the young as well as the old. It is not every day you hear a man say, "He is a sweet man; I recognized that the first time I met him." He never felt the need to be with others to be happy but enjoyed our many friends at the same time.

I never knew I was capable of loving anyone as much as I loved Fred. We could just sit by the fire and read and feel such closeness.

We ended the service with my favorite songs created on a CD by our friend Ed Scott. "Time To

Say Goodbye," sung by Sarah Brightman, "No One Like You," also sung by Sarah, and "Be Not Afraid" and "Here I Am, Lord."

Thank you, God, for twelve wonderful years with the most wonderful man in the world, and thank you for sending him to me to be loved because it would have been a shame for someone so special to go through what he went through and to die alone.

Fred was not one to tell me how much he loved me, but he sure found cards to express his feelings, and I loved them.

> Front cover
> I'm Glad You're My Wife
>
> Betsy,
> Sharing life with you has grown
> so familiar and comfortable that
> I sometimes forget to tell you
> how much it all means to me…
> how wonderful you are… and
> how very much I love you.
>
> Happy Valentine's Day.
> With all my love,
> Fred

Another at Christmas:
Front Cover
I Love My Wife

Inside

> I love the smile that lights your face,
> Love the warmth of your embrace,
> I love the voice that says, "I Care,"
> Love each little joy we share.
> I love your way of being sweet,
> Of making my life so complete,
> Of understanding, as you do…
> I love you just because you're you!

Merry Christmas

After Fred's death, I got the idea to write a book in hopes of helping others going through the same thing. I called it *Pathway to Heaven*. It is an idea whose time is long overdue. There is no greater need than to comfort someone in their final days of life. The purpose is to guide you through the process. You only get one chance; get it right.

Teaching children how to make boxes out of greeting cards, I came across another one of Fred's cards and want to record it here.

To My Wife on Her Birthday

Dearest Betsy,
Each moment that
I spend with you
I know I love you more,
Each day brings more fulfillment
than I knew the day before,
Each year just adds more beauty
and more meaning to my life—
I love you and I need you,
I'm so glad that you're my wife.

Downsizing—Moving on with Life

THE TIME COMES WHEN ONE should downsize, and that happened to me in 2019. I had been writing articles in the *Desert Sun*, the local newspaper in Palm Springs, California, and this particular one got my attention. Friends were saving their articles for me so I could share them with my family living on the East Coast. No one wanted to part with this one because it related to them, and they needed to reread it. I had sold our home in the mountains in 2014 but still owned a home in Palm Desert, and if I should die here in California, my children would have a heck of a job getting rid of all my stuff—forty years of stuff. Even though I was not a collector and gave constantly, it is still a big job. I'd like to share that article with you here.

Some years ago I read "What did you do with your dash?"

The dash being the space between the date you were born and the date you died. We need to give more thought to the quality of our lives to the very end and live until we die. Long-term care should not just be a financial figure; it should represent comfort in a loving environment.

There are stages in life. The first stage we are young, in school, either on the phone or in front of a mirror, know everything, got the cat by the tail, and think we are on top of the world. Parents are old-fashioned and don't know anything.

In the second stage, we marry, have children, and become responsible individuals, or so we like to think.

Then the third and final stage kicks in. As we grow older, we fear change, afraid of what we don't know. We can live, or we can exist; it's up to us. We need to ask ourselves who am I and what do I need to live a happy life? Whether you realize it or not, you need people. Remember the song "People?" People who need people are the luckiest people in the world. I love that song, and Barbara Streisand sings it like none other.

You lost your mate, the love of your life. The most universal urge we all share is to be happy. To wake up each morning in a state of bliss. Bliss is being happy for no reason; it's sharing what you had with others. It's listening to their stories. Reminiscing is a way of reliving your life.

Don't stop living; you have so much to offer. As I sit here writing this, knowing how I fight with all my electronic devices each day, I want you to realize, life is more comfortable in some respects, and this is one of them. We have assisted living facilities now, and you need to think about where you want to spend the rest of your life while you are able to make that decision. Visit the different facilities and take notes.

When you wake up in the morning, jump out of bed, see yourself for who you are, who you want to be. Start each day with love in your heart. Today I will make everyone I come into contact with feel special, either by a compliment or a smile.

If you are able to volunteer, do it. Volunteering will do more for you than it will do for others. Every business is an opportunity to help. Helping others helps you. Happiness comes from thinking more about others than ourselves.

If you are living in a country club not utilizing the benefits offered, you are wasting your money and your life. Downsizing is healthy and can be fun. We always need something to look forward to and remember happiness does not come from stuff.

Friends are presents we give ourselves. Don't waste your final years alone; share them with the world. You are never too old to make new friends, and you have a lot to offer.

When you ask God to take over your life, direct your path, he does, and he even proves it to you.

Living here in Mount Pleasant, South Carolina, now there are a few things I really miss from my home in California. Before going to bed each night, I went to my dining room window, looked up to the sky, and there was a star, shining ever so brightly, and if there wasn't a star shining there when I arrived, one appeared shortly thereafter. I would laugh out loud, knowing God saw me there looking for my star, and he sent it. It gave me pleasure to stand there and thank God for all that had happened during the course of that day. I learned years ago, the more I am grateful for, the more I get to be grateful for. Thank you, God, for my star; I love it.

In my *Jesus Calling* book one day I read, "Look for a star of guidance in your own life, and be willing to follow wherever I lead. I am the light from on high that dawns upon you to guide your feet into the way of Peace." I have a new star here, but it is in the west; it's Jupiter, and it will be there until the end of May—or so Siri tells me.

God's Message to Me

I KNOW I'M IN THE right place; I prayed about it and asked God to direct my path and not let me make a mistake. Wanting to get back to the East Coast, where all my family lives, to make it easier for them to travel up and down the coast instead of across the country, my thought was to move to Augusta, Georgia, where I could play golf and get to enjoy the azaleas and rhododendron. Just one of the things I enjoy so much while watching the Masters golf tournament each year. To my surprise, Charleston popped up on my computer screen. Remembering that Fred and I had honeymooned here and thinking it was nice and the climate was nice, I decided to check it out. I love being near the water, and there is no shortage of water here.

Sitting on my third-floor balcony with my son, Thomas, and daughter-in-law, Dinah Mae, to my surprise, I found that one of the trees in front of the lake has a perfect cross growing out the top of it. My first thought was, *OK, God, I got your message; I am right where you want me.* There have been so many holy moments, so many stories to tell.

On my trip to Charleston, I was picked up by a black man driving for Uber. He told me how depressed he had been, and he sold his gun for fear he would use it because he has people depending on him for their survival. At the end of the trip, I gave him one of my prayer cards. He read it and gave me the biggest bear hug I have had in a long time. Anyone seeing this would have wondered, *What is the old black man doing hugging that old white woman?*

It was six o'clock in the morning, and I was going to the airport, and another Uber driver picked me up. This time, it was a mother of three. We talked about the importance of communication. Do you talk to your children every day when they return from school and ask them about their day? It is so important because they may have had their little feelings hurt, and you could comfort them. Bullying is a way of life, and they need to know how to handle it. She was so grateful for our conversation; she gave me a big hug as we were parting.

Leaving church one Sunday morning with my friend Al and having a desire to go to the consignment store, I found the very armoire I had been wanting.

Another time, I held a dream in my heart for a round table for my bedroom. Leaving church again, turning on El Paseo Drive, there was a sign: "Going Out of Business." I went in and there it was, just what I wanted with the exception of the glass for the top, but the salesman instructed us as to where I could find it, and I did.

Driving home from the AAA in Palm Desert, I received a mental message: "Go to the Home Goods store; they have a nightstand you want." There it was, just what I was looking for.

Sitting in church on a Tuesday, I asked God to let me know he was here with me, and in the quiet of the church, it sounded as though someone had entered. I had to look around to be sure there was no one in that church but me. Wanting to visit Carmel before leaving for South Carolina, I remembered Father Lincoln saying he always asks Jesus to ride with him when he goes anywhere. This was going to be a seven-hour drive from my home in Palm Desert to Carmel, and as I backed out of my driveway, I sat for a minute and asked Jesus to ride with me. Good thing I did.

A Head-on Collision Spared

DRIVING ON HIGHWAY 101, A two-lane road, and not wanting to remain behind a large, long-bodied truck, I attempted to pass the truck. I could see cars coming, but they were a long way away. I was side by side with the cabin of this truck. My accelerator was on the floor; I could see I was going to have a head-on collision, and there was nothing I could do to stop it. I have never been so frightened in my life. I could feel the impact.

Just before the collision, both cars jumped out from in front of me like lightning had struck them. I thought it was only one car; I could not see another one behind him. When I arrived at Doris Day's hotel, the Cypress Inn, I went directly to the bar and had a glass of wine. Thank you, Father Lincoln, for sharing that thought with me.

Sitting on the bench by the lake where I live, talking to Jesus, I asked him to let me know he was with me. *Make a fish jump up in this lake.* And a fish jumped up right in front of me.

Why am I sharing all these stories with you? It is because you do not realize you have the power to do the same. I receive so many thoughts from God, and the one I love is my story about sharing a prayer card. Another one is that happiness is contagious; you can spread it, and I can help. Most people have no idea the power they have, if they only allow it to happen. It took me a long time to realize it, but I am never letting it go now.

For a Happy, Peaceful Life

WHY IS MY FAVORITE WORD. I am a *why* person and know there is a reason for all human behavior and a solution to every problem.

Let's confront some of our problems.

First: Why Is Our Birth Rate the Lowest It Has Been in Years?

My thoughts:

There is fear of having a child with preexisting conditions, for one thing.

Seeing children being born without limbs would be enough for me. This child will be dependent on you for the rest of his or her life.

Autism is another; some of these children cannot speak.

Gender dysphoria is another, children feeling they were born to be another sex, not happy being who they are.

So many children are being born with problems, and no one seems to care.

It could be that they are being created from altered sperm.

Having a child reach the teenage years and turning to drugs, alcohol, or gangs, or going to a school to kill others is another fear.

Possible solution:
I think it has a lot to do with pills being used for pleasure.

Pills are for pain, and it is a known fact there is at least one side effect to every pill.

Our pharmaceutical companies have a responsibility to educate people about the drugs they are taking.

Birth control pills are great, but if you want to have a child, you need to know how long you need to wait for your body to get back to normal before conceiving a child.

Conceiving a child in a uterus raging with hormones does not make sense.

Stop believing childhood vaccinations are the problem. When it wasn't a problem before, why would it be now?

Stop messing with God. Healthy sperm in a healthy uterus will create a healthy child.

Second: Why Do People Turn to Drugs, Join Gangs, or Go to Schools to Kill Others?

My thoughts:

- Feelings of worthlessness, depression, and a lack of meaning in their lives
- A lack of self-esteem brought about from a lack of praise
- Being bullied by their parents. Telling anyone to do something is a form of bullying.

We need to know we are loved and that someone cares about us. Did you give birth to have your own slave?

- Feeling unloved. Hugs make a big difference in our lives.

We need to be encouraged to volunteer, do something for others to make us feel good. Encourage them to care about others. Compliments are magic, and young people need them to start at a very young age. I firmly believe they would remove the need for piercings and tattoos. Our young turn to these things for recognition in some form. They confuse a comment for a compliment.

Possible solution:
Is to make your child feel special.

Show an interest in him.

Compliment good behavior.

Ask him to help you with whatever you are doing.

To ask creates a desire to please, it makes him happy to make you happy. Encourage them to learn to dance, play golf, play a musical instrument.

Give them an opportunity to be proud and show off their accomplishments.

How was your day? Tell me about it.

Encourage communication.

You look great in that outfit.

Listen. Don't tell him what to do.

Thank him for helping you, and praise him for doing a great job.

Tell him you appreciate whatever he is doing for you.

Mary wants to know how to get her child to do something without wanting to be paid. She was telling him to wash her car. Ask him to do it, thank him for having done it, and praise him for doing a great job. I promise, he will not want to be paid.

To ask creates a desire to please; to tell is bullying.

Encourage your child to volunteer. Volunteering will do more for us than it does for others. It makes us more interesting people, removes boredom, and could lead to a free education.

Third: Why Are Our Prisons So Full?

My thoughts:

There is a lack of communication skills, social skills, and praise. Skills pump you up and make you feel special.

A young man jumped in front of me as I was leaving the post office, saying, "Let me get that for you." He meant he would get the door. It stopped me in my tracks; that has never happened to me before. I said to him, "Young man, when you get home, I want you to give your mother a big hug from me and tell her I said she is doing a great job." His remark was, "I know. I was raised; I didn't just grow up."

Giving birth is a responsibility.

Raise a child you can be proud of.

Never criticize the behavior of your child; they are an outgrowth of your upbringing.

I'm told that 80 percent of all people wake up with a confrontation in mind. We need to be told to start your day with love in your heart.

Happiness begets happiness.

People argue and fight. People need to know to argue is an act of ignorance and is a waste of time. If they read Dale Carnegie's book *How to Win Friends and Influence People*, they would know that all they want is to say what they feel is right and why they feel that way. And if the other person agrees with them, fine; if not, that's OK too.

You don't have to be right.

The person with no communications skills is the person most likely to argue; he has no thoughts of his own to contribute to the conversation, so he contradicts what you say for no reason.

Our tolerance level is too low. We need to be taught to always have a sympathetic desire to see the other person's viewpoint and to always be ready to say we are sorry.

We never know what another person is going through. Grieving comes in many forms: the loss of a parent, a sibling, or an animal, or just having our feelings hurt. You cannot see pain, and because we cannot feel their pain, we should treat everyone in a loving way. At some point in our lives, we will all experience physical and emotional pain, so let's make it a practice to keep our tolerance level as high as we possibly can.

Everyone is entitled to their own thoughts,

especially when it comes to religion and politics. It is never a good idea to push your agenda or ideas on others. These subjects are best kept to oneself, unless you are part of the same organization. It is not worth losing your friends over your political views. Nothing can ever be unsaid or undone, so give thought to what you are about to do or say. Select your words carefully.

Possible solutions:

Words are not always taken the way they are meant.

When this happens, say, "I'm not sure what you mean. Can you explain your thinking?"

Written words have no personality, no facial expression, and no tone of voice, so they must be selected very carefully.

When you have a problem with someone, don't blame them. Start with yourself, and ask yourself, *What did I do or say to make that person react in that manner?*

We have choices in life; we can choose to be offended or not offended. It's all about our attitude.

Deepak Chopra tell us in his book *The Seven Spiritual Laws of Success* that everything that is happening in your life at this moment is a result of the choices you have made in the past. Is this decision I am about to make going to bring happiness to me and all those around me?

If not, I shouldn't do it.

My message to my children was, "Don't do anything you wouldn't do if I were standing right beside you, and you will be never go wrong." I also asked God to watch over them and not let them do anything to hurt themselves or anyone else. It works and removes fear.

Fourth: Why Are So Many Marriages Falling Apart?

My thoughts:

Because we marry for the wrong reasons.

We think this person is going to make us happy.

God gave us special feelings to let us know we are in love.

Love is not just a word; it's a feeling. My definition of love is "the desire to do with and for without expecting anything in return because it gives you pleasure to bring happiness to this person."

Does it give you pleasure to bring happiness to this person? Is this someone you are proud of?

Best quotes about a perfect marriage:

"A perfect marriage is two imperfect people that never give up on each other."

A friend on her third marriage tells me, "He doesn't make me happy." Did you get married so you would have someone to make you happy? Are you entitled to happiness? Did someone sprinkle stardust on you when you were born and tell you that everyone will do all in their power to make you happy the rest of your life?

Do you know real, lasting happiness comes from bringing happiness to others? No one is responsible for your happiness but you. It is true; we harvest what we sow.

How do we find happiness?

We start by thinking more about others than ourselves. We show concern by asking questions and listening.

Did you marry your best friend?

Can you sit quietly on a riverbank and feel the warmth and love without saying a word? Was your friendship deeper than drinking and hanging out?

Are you comfortable talking about everything, and is this someone you can cry with and someone who supports your life goals and believes in you?

Do you know arguing kills love?

Nothing can ever be unsaid or undone. You can say you are sorry, but it is still there. Communication is the key to living in harmony with others, and you don't have to be right.

Marriages break up because one or the other person is getting their needs met by someone else.

Foreplay starts when you get out of bed in the morning, not when you go to bed at night. What is he getting from another that he is not getting from you? Appreciation? Gratitude?

You know whatever it is you want from another, you must give it first.

Here are some magic phrases I believe will keep love in your relationship:

> *What's on your agenda for the day?*
> *Would you like me to help you with that?*
> *Thank you for being so special.*
> *You look great in that outfit.*
> *Thank you for helping me.*
> *I really appreciate all you do for me.*
> *I am so proud of you.*
> *Good job!*
> *How was your day? Tell me about it.*
> *This is a great dinner; thank you for making this.*

Someone showing an interest in us and appreciating what we do makes us feel special. To appreciate will set you apart from the rest of the world, and a compliment is a moment of happiness in another person's life.

My first marriage ended in divorce because we never appreciated each other, complimented each other, and never said thank you. We married to be getting married.

Remember, words are not always taken the way they were meant, and our tone of voice plays a large role in our delivery. We need to see things from others' points of view and always be ready to say we are sorry.

Possible solutions:

Your happiness does not come from stuff; it comes from thinking more about others than yourself.

Start seeing this person with your heart and not just your eyes.

Show compassion, caring and sharing yourself with another will bring about a tremendous change in you.

Praise and compliments have a lot in common; they are both about value and worth. People are so fast to complain and so slow to compliment.

A compliment can bring about change in another person.

If someone is behaving destructively and you want them to change, you can praise them in ways that make them want to change. Words are so powerful in this respect. Stay away from the three Cs: criticizing, condemning, and complaining. If you see a problem, think it out, and come up with a solution, then present the problem and your ideas to correct it.

Good communication is reminiscing about the good times you have had together and bringing out the best in one another. Start communicating your feelings, and stop killing love.

Wake up each morning in a state of bliss. You ask, "What is a state of bliss?" It's being happy for no reason.

Remember, if you have someone in your life, you are lucky; some people go to their graves without having experienced love. Don't take it for granted; appreciate it.

Happiness is contagious; you can spread it, and I can help!

Fifth: Why Are So Many People Just Existing and Not Living?

My thoughts:

Because they don't know any better.

I didn't know how to live until I was seventy-five years old. We need a manual to help us get the most out of life. Everything comes with a set of operating instructions, and people are no exception. Most people think happiness comes from stuff: a new car, a new house, drugs, a baby, a new dress, material things. That's why you see hoarders. They keep shopping until they have no space left to walk in their homes. Stuff wears out or (as with drugs) off.

They don't know volunteering will do so much for them.

They don't know they have the ability to create their own happiness.

They don't know that if they can see it, and they can feel it, and they can believe it, it is entirely possible.

Their thinking is, *I'm just trying to make it through the day,* and that's exactly what they do: just make it through the day.

They are poor because all they think about is how poor they are.

Possible solutions:

Sit quietly for fifteen minutes each day and meditate. Hold a picture of yourself in your mind of who you are now and who you want to become. It will happen.

Start giving of yourself.

Volunteer; it will bring so much happiness to you.

Start your day with a positive affirmation:

The quality of my life depends only on me.

I peacefully allow my life to unfold into overflowing abundance.

Today I will think of the many achievements I am going to accomplish in the future that are vastly superior to anything I have done in the past.

I have an attitude of gratitude.

I will ignore any doubts in my head.

I am filled with peaceful awareness.

I am consciously aware that my future is generated by the choices I am making every moment of my life.

Every morning, I will jump out of bed and tell myself, *Something good is going to happen to me today. I'll look for it, and it will happen.*

I radiate love wherever I go.

Invite God to come in, take over your life, direct your path, and fill that empty space with inner peace. You will never be the same.

Sixth: Why Are So Many People in Debt?

My thoughts:

Most of us have never been taught money management skills. We buy things we don't need because we find stuff comforting.

We are depressed and lack meaning in our lives.

We have never purchased a ledger, listed our income, recorded our financial obligations on paper, and tried to live within our means.

It is so easy to purchase with a credit card.

There is no meaning in our lives, so we shop.

Possible solutions:

Purchase a ledger, and list your financial obligations.

Record them each month. Seeing it on paper helps.

Ask yourself, *Do I need this?* If not, don't buy it.

I love to shop but do not buy anything I do not need. I tell myself I am treating my eyes. When I see something I really like, I tell myself that if I still feel the same way in a couple of days and cannot forget it, I'll buy it. With this thinking, you are removing impulse buying.

I never liked having to take things back because I changed my mind.

We buy because we are lonely, so get involved in something you enjoy doing.

Seventh: Why Do We Have Wars?

My thoughts:

A complete lack of communication skills. It's the result of so many people just growing up without skills of any kind, with no compassion for another.

No one is making an attempt to examine the situation.

Find out what they want.

Why are you willing to die?

People are being bullied all their lives with their parents telling them what to do.

So much hate builds up in them, and they feel a power struggle to push others around. This has to be the result of being criticized, abused verbally, sexually, and emotionally all your life and being told you are worthless and will never amount to anything.

Two hundred men showed up on *The Oprah Winfrey Show* with pictures of themselves at the age they were sexually abused.

Something needs to be done about this.

Possible solutions:

When we see this in our youth at a young age, get them help.

Set up an ongoing counseling system in our schools, and bring children in to discuss their lives. What's going on at home?

Create a hotline that can be called at any time, day or night. This way we will be able to catch it at an early age.

Children being abused, verbally and sexually, cannot function at the rate others can. We do this in corporations; let's do it in our schools. Call it a review to see if you need help.

Encourage retired people, parents, and school-teachers to offer this help to the school system.

Encourage parents to teach their children compassion, to be the person others want to emulate.

Stress communication skills in our schools. An academic education is worthless without communication skills.

Teach our men and women how to avoid a war instead of how to run one.

To argue and fight is an act of ignorance, a waste of time, and a lack of communication skills.

Eighth: Why Are So Many People on Medications?

My thoughts:

They are stressed and depressed and lack meaning in their lives.

They believe everything their doctors tell them.

Some people almost wear it as a badge of honor: "How wonderful! My doctor loves me so much; he has me taking all these pills."

They need to take their life in their own hands and ask questions, and check the medicines that are being recommended for them.

Every pill has at least one side effect. People are taking as many as fifteen pills a day. Some of my friends are taking so many pills; their hands shake so badly they can hardly get a glass up to their mouths.

Doctors have recommended medications for me that were not needed and would have done harm to my body. My general practitioner recommended I take Fosamax for my bones. When I asked her why, she said it was because I am past menopause and needed to protect my bones. I took it for two months and requested a test to see if I really needed it. It is a little pill that you must take each morning sitting up and wait for a half hour before eating or drinking anything.

I did not need to take this pill. My test showed I have the bones of a twenty-year-old, and the attending physician told me he would have to see at least one hundred patients before he would find one with bones as good as mine. Had I continued to take that pill, it would have destroyed my bones. I'm told by people taking this pill that their bones become brittle and break for no reason at all.

The same doctor wanted to put me on medicine for diabetes. They get you on that one for life. Her message to me was, "You are on the verge of becoming a full-blown diabetic." My response was, "I don't take pills, so we will wait for a month or two, and I'll come back to be tested again."

I knew I had eaten a whole pumpkin pie in a short period of time. I love those Costco pumpkin pies! Sure enough, when I went back for the test, I was fine; the pie had passed through. That's only two experiences; I had more with different doctors. Never take their word for anything. Get a second opinion, or do your own research.

Possible solutions:

I created a list of questions to ask your doctor and have shared it with many people and want to share it with you. Print it out, and take it with you when you go to see a doctor.

- Is this medicine necessary, and why do you think I need it?
- What are the side effects of this medication?
- Is this surgery really necessary?
- Are there other options?
- What are the risks and side effects?
- What are the benefits?
- Are there less invasive treatments possible?
- What happens if I don't do anything?
- How successfully can the surgery relieve my symptoms?
- How long do you think it will take me to recover?
- Would it be wise for me to spend the night in the hospital?

- What is my chance of contacting a staph infection?
- What is the risk of contamination?
- How long can I expect to be on this medication, and what are the side effects of this medication?
- Pain pills are constipating. Do you think Tylenol will work?
- Should I apply heat or ice to the area?
- What is the worst-case scenario?
- I should contact you immediately if what happens?

Lord, let your healing spirit rest upon me today.

Having a desire to help, heal, and comfort brought all those questions, thoughts, and possible solutions to me. If you share them, maybe we can all start living holy moments every day too.

Birds in My Life

IT IS DIFFICULT FOR US to believe that we can die, be buried, and live on without our flesh and bones, but I am here to tell you that happens. My husband Fred had a fondness for birds and taught me a lot about them. We cherished any opportunity to see a red-tailed hawk in flight or nesting in the trees at the driving range of our country club.

On my way to the kitchen one morning, a big red-tailed hawk landed on the little gate on our patio. I froze in total shock and just stood there looking at him. This big bird was just sitting there turning his head ever so slowly from one side to the other as if to say, "Am I on the right patio?" He wanted to be sure he had the right house. I knew it was the spirit of Fred, telling me he is OK. I wish I had taken a picture of him. I was so afraid if I moved, he would fly away. Anyone reading this is going to think I am making it up, but I promise you, I am not making any of this up.

A Chick-a-dee Arrived

IT WAS MAY OF 2008, and I had arrived at our home in Plumas Pines for the first time after the death of Fred. For a couple of days, a little bird had been trying to get into the house. He started at the den window, and when I told a friend, he said, "It's Fred, and he wants to get at that computer." This little bird had been to the den, kitchen, and bathroom windows. He kept flying up the window, fluttering his wings, and pecking the window on his way down. It was a chickadee, and they didn't usually arrive that early in the spring.

He finally sat still on the little metal strip on the bathroom window, and I took his picture, first from a distance because I was afraid he would fly away, but I kept walking closer and closer and even stepped in the bathtub and got right in his face and took a picture of him. After that, he flew away and has not been back.

It was Kentucky Derby time, and a horse with a bird name was running in the eleventh race: Summer Bird. Could it be my chickadee? I had to go to Fantasy Springs in Indio to place a bet on this horse. The chickadee arrived in the summer, so that was my clue.

I placed a bet of forty dollars on Summer Bird to win. Sitting in my car looking over the program before returning home, I saw there was another horse with a bird in its name and it was, "Mine That Bird," and that turned out to be the winner.

I hope you have the kind of day that feels like God made it just for you.

What would you do if I told you that what you do this week could change the world? Maybe one of you will give a statement of encouragement to someone who will see something in herself that she hadn't before and, in turn, will befriend another who was on the verge of giving up on life…

Maybe one of you will be talking with a friend about the difference God has made in your life and not even realize that another is listening with an open heart. Or maybe you will be moved to volunteer and realize it makes you a better, more interesting person to be around.

Some of your actions may be big, bold, and

courageous. Others may be small, hardly notice-able, yet they all have the potential to ripple out, affecting countless lives.

Who knows what difference what you say and do will make in God's world? Hopefully, you have learned you are the master of your life.

When you ask God to take over your life, di-rect your path, and use you to bring happiness to others, you will be a much happier person. Your whole world will open up.

One thing we know for sure: God does not push himself on us; he must be invited in.

> I give you this one thought to keep,
> I am with you still, I do not sleep.
> I am a thousand winds that blow,
> I am the diamond glints on snow,
> I am the sunlight on ripened grain,
> I am the gentle autumn rain.
> When you awaken in the
> morning hush, I am the swift,
> uplifting rush of quiet birds in circled flight.
> I am the soft stars that shine at night.
> Do not think of me as gone.
> I am with you still in each new dawn.

—AUTHOR UNKNOWN

www.ingramcontent.com/pod-product-compliance
Lightning Source LLC
Chambersburg PA
CBHW032025050726
47590CB00006B/2308